SCANDALS, SIEGES

ESSEX
GHOSTS & LEGENDS

PAMELA BROOKS

HALSGROVE

First published in Great Britain in 2010

British Library Cataloguing-in-Publication Data
A CIP record for this title is available from the British Library

ISBN 978 0 85704 011 4

HALSGROVE
Halsgrove House,
Ryelands Industrial Estate,
Bagley Road, Wellington, Somerset TA21 9PZ
Tel: 01823 653777   Fax: 01823 216796
email: sales@halsgrove.com

Part of the Halsgrove group of companies
Information on all Halsgrove titles is available at: www.halsgrove.com

Printed and bound by Short Run Press Ltd., Exeter

Contents

For my father,
John Roy Sewell,
with love

Preface

There are some incredibly beautiful ruins in Essex, and there are fascinating human stories behind the stones: stories of sieges and bloodshed, of ghosts and spooky creatures, and of scandals among the monks and nuns.

Although there are more castles and priories in the county than I've included here, not all have legends or tales attached; I've focused on the ones with the most interesting stories. I hope you enjoy reading these stories as much as I've enjoyed researching them.

This is also the place where I would like to say thank you. First of all to my husband Gerard and my children Christopher and Chloë, for their enthusiasm in going exploring and visiting all the sites covered in this book (as well as visiting churches where many, many generations of my family were baptised, married and buried – and especial thanks to Gerard for taking over the driving and putting up with my habit of directing him down very narrow lanes), and to my uncle and aunt, Richard and Chrissy Camp, for supplying cups of tea and suggestions. To Dot Lumley, my wonderful agent, as always for her support, encouragement and wisdom. To Simon Butler at Halsgrove, for giving me the chance to tell these stories. And, last but not least, very grateful thanks to Norfolk County Libraries for their help in finding texts.

Pamela Brooks
June 2010

Ashingdon

The Battle of Ashingdon was fought on 18 October 1016, at Assandun, between the armies of Edmund II of England (aka Edmund Ironside) and Canute the Great of Denmark.

The story behind the battles starts almost three years earlier, when Sweyn Forkbeard, the king of Denmark, forced Ethelred from the throne and became the king of England on Christmas Day 1013. However, Sweyn died five weeks later. Sweyn's eldest son, Harald II, was proclaimed king of Denmark, and his younger son, Cnut (hereafter written as 'Canute') claimed the English throne – but the ruling council of English nobles refused to accept Canute as king and said that they wanted Ethelred brought back from exile and restored to the throne.

By 1015, Canute invaded England and occupied Essex and Northumbria. He besieged London in 1016; meanwhile, Ethelred died and his son Edmund was proclaimed king. Edmund left London to gather troops, but Canute's army intercepted him in Essex at Assandun (thought to be either Ashingdon, near the Crouch estuary, although some historians think that Assandun was further north in the county at Ashdon, near Saffron Walden).

Canute's forces were based on the hill at Canewdon while Edmund's forces camped at Ashingdon. The attack was a surprise, and the English army was slaughtered. The *Anglo-Saxon Chronicle* has a brief account of the battle, saying that

Ashingdon Mount, where Edmund's forces are thought to have camped. Photograph by author.

Ealdorman Eadric was the first to run away, with the Magonsæte (who were from the Welsh borders with Herefordshire and Shropshire). The *Encomium Emmae Reginae* goes further and puts the blame firmly on Eadric Streona, saying that he ran away not because he was frightened, but because he'd made a secret deal with the Danes.

The *Anglo-Saxon Chronicle* lists the men killed in the battle:

> There was Bishop Eadnoth killed, and Abbot Wulfsige, and Ealdorman Ælfric, and Godwine, the ealdorman of Lindsey, and Ulfcetel of East Anglia, and Æthelweard, son of Ealdorman Æthelsige, and all the nobility of England was there destroyed.

After the battle, Edmund met Canute at Ola's Island in the River Severn, where they agreed a treaty saying that Edmund would rule Wessex and Canute would control the rest of England north of the Thames. The deal was that when one of them died, the other would rule that territory, and the ruling king's sons would then be the heirs to the throne.

Edmund died a month later on 30 November (and William of Malmesbury said that Eadric was responsible, and bribed two servants to stick a knife in Edmund's bowels – rather horribly, while he was going to the toilet). As a result, Canute became the ruler of England.

Tradition has it that Canute built a minster at Ashingdon to atone for the number of dead at Assandun, and that St Michael's church in Ashingdon sits on the site of the minster.

Ashingdon village sign, commemorating the Battle of Assandun, 1016. Photograph by author.

Spooks: The Soldiers from the Battle of Ashingdon

Tradition has it that the moans of the dying soldiers can still be heard on the hill, and that the blood ran so thickly at the battle that no grass grows there. (However, the picture below shows that the hill most certainly has grass on it!).

St Michael's church, Ashingdon. Photograph by author.

Spooks: The Witches and Ghosts of Canewdon

Nearby at Canewdon, a 'grey lady' has been seen on moonless nights, travelling through the west gate towards the river; she may be linked with a witch mentioned by folklorist Eric Maple, who wrote about 'Witch Hart' who lived in Latchingdon in the sixteenth century, stole a bell from the church and tried to bring it back to the witches of Canewdon. So the story goes, her boat was a wash-tub and her oars were feathers; she was seen by a waterman, but she cast a spell to make him forget. Apparently she drowned, and her ghost haunts the river and sea-wall.

There's also a rather tempting legend that says if you run round the church three times on 31 October, you travel through time.

There's a tradition that there are always six witches at Canewdon, 'three in six and three in cotton' (i.e. three rich women and three poor ones). Rosa Pye of Canewdon was accused of bewitching Richard Snow's one-year-old daughter to death in 1580 but was acquitted.

St Nicholas' church, Canewdon. Photograph by author.

Barking Abbey

Barking Abbey (OS map reference TQ439 834) is the remains of a Benedictine abbey dedicated to St Mary. The only remaining building is the curfew or fire bell gate, which was rebuilt in 1640. The grounds of the old abbey were officially opened as a conservation area in May 1975 and the park is open to the public. The curfew tower is occasionally open to the public on special heritage days, when the stone rood dating from the eleventh or twelfth century can be seen in the upper room. Some of the finds from the excavations are on display in St Margaret's church.

Remains of gateway at Barking Abbey; plate from Thomas Kitson Cromwell's Excursions Through Essex, 1818-9.

Curfew tower, aka remains of gateway at Barking Abbey.
Photograph by author.

The Beginnings of the Abbey

The abbey was originally founded around 666 by Erkenwald, the bishop of London. Bede, writing 20 or so years later, described the foundation:

> When Sebbi... ruled the East Saxons, Theodore [Archbishop of Canterbury] appointed over them Earconwald to be their bishop in the city of London... before he was made bishop [he] built 2 goodly monasteries, 1 for himself [at Chertsey in Surrey], the other for his sister Ethelburga... in the province of the East Saxons at the place that is named in Bericingum.

9

Gardens surrounding remains of Barking Abbey. Photograph by author.

Ethelburga became the first abbess of Barking. It was said to be the first nunnery established in England, and Erkenwald sent to France for the nun Hildelitha to come and instruct the English novices. Although the charter that was allegedly made by Erkenwald is not thought to be authentic, there is a charter of the abbey by Holdeldred, the father of King Sebbi, which dates from the time of the abbey's foundation, and this is one of the oldest abbey charters in existence.

The Miracle of St Erkenwald

Erkenwald died at Barking in April 693, and a huge row broke out over where he should be buried. The nuns at Barking wanted him to be buried there, as he was the founder of the abbey; the monks at Chertsey had a similar claim; and the citizens of London claimed that, as he was their bishop, he should be buried there.

The Londoners won the argument because of 'a miracle' (though what form this miracle took isn't explained anywhere!) and took his body from Barking to London. They had to stop at Ilford because of flooding, so they knelt and prayed for a miracle; immediately, the waters parted, so they were able to take his body safely to Stratford. Finally, they interred his body in St Paul's cathedral and put up a shrine to him on the east wall.

Fire and Refoundation

The abbey was attacked by the Danes in 870; rather gruesomely, the invaders burned the building with the nuns still inside, and the nuns all died in the fire. The abbey was deserted for about a century, and then was refounded in 970 as a Benedictine double house (i.e. a monastery and a nunnery, both under the rule of the abbess). However, excavations at Barking have revealed no foundations earlier than the twelfth century, so it's probable that the earlier nunnery was built on a slightly different site.

King Edgar gave the nunnery to Wulfhildis, a nun from Wilton, in reparation for 'violence offered to her'; James Sergeant Storer, writing in 1807, says it was because Edgar violated the nun's chastity. Wulfhildis ruled the nunnery until the reign of Ethelred, Edgar's son. The priests at Barking were jealous of her and often fought with her; finally, they persuaded Elfrida (Edgar's widow and Ethelred's mother) to oust her. Wulfhildis then retired to a nunnery at Horton, Devonshire.

Meanwhile, Elfrida ruled Barking as the abbess for 20 years, until she became ill. She had a dream of Ethelburga, the original abbess; as a result, she decided that Wulfhildis should be reinstated as abbess. Wulfhildis ruled the abbey for the next seven years, later moving to London to avoid the Danes where she died.

The royal family had close connections with Barking. William the Conqueror spent his first new year there in 1066/7, while he finished building fortifications in London, and it's thought that the northern earls (Edwin of Mercia and Morcar of Northumbria) submitted to him at Barking Abbey.

Until 1214, the king had right to appoint the abbess at Barking. Maud, the queen of Henry I, was abbess of Barking before her death in 1118, and Matilda, the wife of Stephen, was abbess in 1136. However, the pope pressured King John to grant the right of free election to English monastic houses. Barking was one of the first to do this, in 1215, though the king did step in and say that under no circumstances were the nuns to allow the sister of Robert Fitzwalter to be elected. This was probably because King John was busy fighting Fitzwalter elsewhere – and even besieged Fitzwalter at Binham Priory in Norfolk. (See also Little Dunmow on page 77 for an account of the feuds between John and Fitzwalter.)

Miracles and Plagues

According to Bede, miracles occurred at Barking during the time of the plague. As Barking was a double monastery, the nuns needed to be kept separate from the monks – and that included burials as well as everyday living. The abbess knelt and prayed for guidance about where the nuns should be buried; that night, a great light shone on the south side of the monastery, which was allegedly brighter than the light of day, and then withdrew again. The abbess said that this was the sign she'd asked for, and the nuns were buried on that spot from then on.

There was also a three-year-old boy called Esion, who was being brought up in the abbey and was taught by the nuns. He died from the plague; on his deathbed, he called out three times to his favourite nun, called Eadgith. The story goes, at that very moment she developed the plague, too; dying the same day.

Scandal: Visitations

In 1279, the abbey clearly wasn't running as it should have been, because the nuns received a set of injunctions from Archbishop Peckham. He told the nuns that they were not to cut divine offices short, they had say matins at midnight, and compline had to be said on time every day to stop the nuns chattering. He also said that children were not allowed to perform the mystery plays, because it would turn the praise of God into a game; instead, the nuns had to do all the acting. The wine at the altar was sour, and the archbishop insisted that better wine should be used. He added that nobody should go into the parlour to talk after sunset, and the abbey gates had to be locked then.

Discipline was clearly a problem, because he specifically stated that men weren't allowed in the nuns' rooms or the offenders would be excommunicated – meaning that they couldn't go to church services, be buried in consecrated ground, or be a party to any legal contracts (which included buying and selling). The Archbishop did allow for some exceptions to the rule, though: if the nun was too ill to be moved, or the infirmary was full, a doctor would be allowed into her room to treat her, and the nun's father, brother or confessor would also be allowed in. Some of the nuns were reported to be disobedient and refused to do unpleasant work; the Archbishop ruled that the abbess had to set a good example, and if any nun refused to do her work three times she had to be sent to the bishop.

In 1308, it was claimed that feasts were kept riotously on certain Sundays and on holidays near the feasts of St Margaret and St Ethelburga. The bishop decreed that the rowdiness had to stop, but even so local landowner Sir John de Massyngburn continued to keep rowdy feast days at the abbey, and three years later the bishop had to tell him off and make further injunctions.

Prison and Politics

Because Barking had close royal links, the abbey often had to give board and lodging to royal servants, as well as to political prisoners. During the wars between England and Scotland, Robert the Bruce's second wife, Elizabeth, was kept prisoner at Barking Abbey between March 1313 and March 1314; she was then moved to Rochester Castle for greater security.

In 1397, Eleanor de Bohun, the Duchess of Gloucester, retired to Barking after her husband Thomas was murdered at Calais (see the full story under Pleshey Castle, page 97). Eleanor returned to Pleshey in 1399 and died there (although some sources say that she died at Barking).

Daily Life

Thomas Kitson Cromwell has some interesting facts about what the cellaress had to provide for the convent:

- to 'bake with elys [eels] on Schere-Thursday' ('Schere-Thursday' was the Thursday after Lady Day, which was 25 March).
- to provide 'a pece of whete and three gallons of milk for frimete [frumenty, a dish made from cracked wheat boiled in milk and sometimes flavoured with spices and almonds; the fourteenth-century poem *Wynnere and Wastoure* describes it served as a 'pottage' or stew with venison] on St Alburgh's (Ethelburgh's) day
- three gallons of gude ale for besons
- marybones [marrow bones] to make white wortys [worts were herbs, usually served boiled then mixed with butter and poured over diced bread – presumably here the jelly from the marrowbones was used instead of clarified butter to make the dish]
- cripsis and crum-kakes at Shroftyde [i.e. cakes using up the milk and eggs that were not allowed to be eaten during Lent]
- conies [rabbits] for the convent at Shroftyde
- twelve stubbe-eles, and nine schaft-eles, to bake on Schere-Thursday
- one potel tyre [i.e. a bottle of strong sweet wine – although it was named after the Syrian seaport of Tyre, it was actually made in Calabria or Sicily] for the abbess the same day, and two gallons of red wyne for the convent
- half a goose for each of the nuns on the feast of the Assumption, and the same on St Alburgh's day
- for every lady a lyverey of sowse at Martinmas, a whole hog's sowse [which consisted of the face, feet, and groin] to serve three ladies.

She also had to pay to every lady in the convent:

- 9d a year for ruschew-silver (money to buy butter)
- 2d for her cripsis and crum-kakes at Shroftyde
- 1½d a week ey-silver (egg-money) from Michaelmas to Allhallows day.
- from that day till Easter 1¾d a week
- and from Easter to Michaelmas 1½d.

Floods

There were bad floods at the beginning of the fourteenth century, which caused great damage to the abbey's possessions and therefore meant the abbey became short of funds. In 1302, abbess Anne de Vere was excommunicated for not paying tithes to the pope. The financial situation continued to be difficult, and in 1319 the abbey was given royal permission to fell 300 oaks to pay for repairs to the buildings.

In 1377, there were major floods along the Thames, which wrecked many of Barking Abbey's possessions. There were further severe floods in 1382 and 1384, even though the nuns had spent more than £2,000 in repairing the banks to avoid further flooding (equivalent to more than three-quarters of a million pounds in modern terms), and in 1409 the abbey was given exemption from paying tithes because the abbess had spent so much money trying to save their lands. At the time it was claimed that the nuns had lost 600 acres of meadow in Dagenham marsh and 120 acres of wheat. They were also given the right to 'impress' labourers – in other words, make them work for nothing to repair the river bank.

Scandal: Rows Between the Abbey and Local Landowners

According to Edward Tuck, in 1462 there was a row between John Rigby, a local landowner, and the abbey. Rigby dug up the pipes on his land that supplied water to the nunnery and broke them, then demanded that the nuns should pay him and his heirs an annual rent of 24 shillings (equivalent to nearly £600 in modern terms) or eight yards of cloth valued at 24 shillings. Catherine de la Pole, the abbess, didn't trust Rigby to stick to the terms of the agreement and thought that he would try to extort yet more money, so she had the abbey's lands searched for a new spring. When one was found at Newbury she had all the old pipes taken up and the new ones were put from the spring to the abbey through lands belonging to the abbey, to make sure they could avoid future litigation from neighbouring landowners.

The End of the Abbey

Barking Abbey surrendered to the king on 14 November 1539. The abbess, Dorothy Barley, was given a pension of 200 marks a year (one of the two largest pensions given to an abbess – the other being to Elizabeth Zouche, the abbess of Shaftesbury) and 30 other nuns were given smaller sums.

After the suppression of the monasteries, the buildings at Barking were demolished over the next 18 months and the site was then used as a quarry and a farm. Some of the stone went to Dartford to build the king's new house, and the lead from the roofs went to repair the roof at Greenwich Palace.

Excavations

James Dugdale, writing in 1819, says that during a dig a gold ring and fibula were found, as well as a bone comb decorated with a Saxon horse. Excavations outside the abbey precincts found Saxon workshops and part of a mill and a glass foundry.

Edward Tuck, writing eighty years later, says that Saxon coins were found during excavations, plus quite a few Roman bricks; he suggests that materials from Roman ruins at Uphall were used either as original building materials for the abbey or as part of the repair work.

In 1911, Barking Urban District Council excavated the site, and finds included a stone slab inscribed to Martinus, the first Vicar of Barking (1315-28), the fragment of the shaft of a seventh-century cross (which was probably set up in an open space), plus several floor tiles.

Beeleigh-by-Maldon Abbey

Beeleigh Abbey (OS map reference TL 840 077) is the remains of the abbey, which is now part of a private house. The remains include some of the ranges along the cloisters and chapter house; they date from the early thirteenth century with some sixteenth-century remodelling. Although the abbey is privately owned and there is no access to the general public, it can be seen from the footpath.

The Beginning of the Abbey

The abbey was originally founded in 1180 by Robert (or Roger) Mantell for 13 Premonstratensian canons, and was dedicated to the Blessed Virgin Mary and St Nicholas. The monks moved there from Great Parndon. It was originally called Maldon Abbey, but by the twelfth century it was known as Beeleigh.

Beeleigh Abbey. Photograph by author.

Remains of Beeleigh Abbey; plate from Thomas Kitson Cromwell's Excursions Through Essex, *1818-9.*

Scandals: Visitations

In 1269 there was a row between Reginald, the abbot, and the other occupants of the abbey. The king took the abbey into his protection and installed two custodians, John le Moine and William de Aumbly. Reginald was probably removed from office, because in 1272 Andrew appears as the abbot and the custodians were no longer needed.

The visitations were mostly good, but the monks did commit a few small misdemeanours. In 1482, Thomas Lambe was sentenced to saying the whole psalter within forty days for hitting one of the other monks (though it's not recorded why the fight occurred), and Nicholas Brige was sentenced to one day on bread and water for breaking silence in the cloister. They were all told off because their tonsures were not big enough, and they were also told that if any of them went out of the dormitory without permission after the office of compline had been said, they would be put on bread and water.

Clearly the problem of tonsures remained, because six years later the visitation records again mention that the tonsures weren't big enough – Richard Redman, the bishop of St Asaph, carried out the visitation and said that it 'was not decent to have such abundance of hair'.

The Rebel Abbot

In 1403, Abbot Thomas was involved in the plot against Henry IV to restore Richard II (see the story on page 44 under St John's Abbey, Colchester, for full details). His part in the plot is told in his confession.

Abbot Thomas explained that one of the abbot of Colchester's men came to see him and asked him to go to sing a mass at the abbey; he did so and met two men, William Blithe and Mr Beloyne. Blithe read from a paper, but the abbot couldn't remember what Blithe actually said. Then Blithe came to see the abbot before Clean Lent Sunday, and asked him to send for John Pretilwell to meet a gentleman from London. Pretilwell duly came to mass on the Sunday and spoke to Blithe and the abbot privately in the garden. Blithe said that Richard II was coming out of Scotland, and he had promises of aid from the duke of Orleans and Owen Glendower. He asked the abbot for a horse, spear and harness, but the abbot refused; however, later Blithe asked the abbot to lend him money, and this time the abbot agreed to help.

After that, nothing happened for a while – but then the abbot was woken by one of his servants, saying that 80 men had come to the abbey and lots of men involved with the rebellion were being taken. The abbot fled, and a warrant was issued for his arrest on 5 June. He surrendered and wrote out his confession on 22 June at St Albans. He was granted pardon on 13 November for his part in the rebellion, but was removed from his position as the abbot of Beeleigh.

Scandal: Rows with the Town

There was often tension between the inhabitants of monastic foundations and the nearby townsfolk, and Beeleigh was no exception. In 1487, the bridge at Maldon needed repairs, so the bailiffs ordered trees felled to obtain the wood for repairs. This included trees in the lane leading from Woodham Walter park gate to the brook; Abbot Thomas Scarlot claimed that this belonged to the abbey rather than being common land, so he and the canons took their carts to the area to collect the wood. The bailiffs and townspeople said it was their wood, and refused to let the abbot have any of it. The next ten weeks were spent in a legal row, but eventually it was proved that the lane had been a boundary for the town since well before the abbey was built, and the wood belonged to the townsfolk.

The End of the Abbey

The abbey was dissolved in 1536. The Earl of Essex wanted Beeleigh, but didn't get it; the abbey went to Sir John Gates, the Sheriff of Essex, who was beheaded for treason at the Tower of London on 22 August 1553 for his part in the plot to put Lady Jane Grey on the throne.

The chapter house and the calefactory (warming house) remain. The abbey became a farmhouse in the eighteenth and nineteenth centuries, and was restored in the early twentieth century for Captain F. W. Grantham. In 1943, Mr W. A. Foyle of Foyle's Bookshop in Charing Cross Road bought the abbey; he retired two years later and turned the building into a huge library. His daughter Christina took it over when he died in 1963; many of the books (including Shakespeare First Folios and medieval illuminated texts) were sold at auction after her death for £12.6m. His grandson Christopher Foyle owns the abbey and is continuing restoration work.

The Saint of Beeleigh

Matthew Paris, a Benedictine monk at St Albans who wrote the *Chronica Majora* in the thirteenth century, refers to St Roger Niger of Bileye (Beeleigh), whose heart was enshrined in the high altar. Roger was born in Beeleigh in about 1175 and was educated at the abbey. He became a canon of St Paul's, was promoted to the post of Archdeacon of Colchester in 1218, and then finally became Bishop of London in 1229. Matthew Paris described him as 'a very reverend man, religious, learned, painful in preaching, eloquent, a great house-keeper, of very gentle and courteous behaviour'. Allegedly Roger was once preaching at St Paul's Cathedral when lightning struck the building; everyone else fled, but he carried on. He was equally determined in political life, clashing with Henry III and threatening to excommunicate him. He also had rows with Pope over the collection of papal tithes.

Roger died on 29 September 1241 and was buried in St Paul's Cathedral; there was an eclipse of the sun as he was buried, leading to rumours of miracles at his grave. He was canonised in 1249; his heart was buried at Beeleigh, which became a pilgrimage site and was visited by Edward I and Eleanor of Castile in 1289.

At the dissolution of the monasteries, Roger's heart disappeared; however, during excavations in 2002, a strange stone effigy was found in a ditch, with two hands cupped round a heart. It's very tempting to think that this could this be Roger's.

Spooks

There's meant to be a recurring ghost at Beeleigh Abbey on either 11 or 22 August, which stands in a corner of the James Room. It's thought to be either a monk or the ghost of John Gate, who had bought the abbey in 1537 and was executed in 1553 for supporting Lady Jane Grey's claim to the throne. One former owner of the abbey allegedly slept in the room and was woken at 3am by something shaking the bed; her arm became very painful, and when a doctor looked at her arm the next day he said that it looked like the bite of a tropical insect.

Tunnels

As with many of the monastic buildings in East Anglia, there is a rumour of a secret tunnel running from the abbey. In Beeleigh's case, the tunnel is meant to go to All Saints Church in Maldon, although it no longer exists – and most of the alleged tunnels at monastic sites turn out to be simple drainage culverts.

There's a story that, some years ago, archaeologists discovered the entrance to the tunnel; there was too much rubble for them to go in and explore, so one of them sent their dog in. The dog later appeared in the abbey cellar, barking.

Berden Priory

Berden Priory (OS map reference TL4623 3021) was an Augustinian priory dedicated to St John the Evangelist. It was founded by the Rochefords – the lords of the manor of Berden – in the twelfth century. There are no visible remains of the priory. Although there is a farmhouse in Berden called Berden Priory, the building dates from the late sixteenth century, and the architectural historian Nikolaus Pevsner says that it was probably built before Elizabeth I's visit in 1578.

The priory probably began as a hospital, and a midsummer fair was granted to them in 1214.

Fire

The church, cloister, refectory, dormitory, infirmary, hall and nearly all the other buildings were burnt to the ground in the late thirteenth century. On 4 March, 1308, twenty-one bishops promised forty days' indulgence to all who would help the rebuilding of the priory or make gifts to it of ornaments and other things, and the priory was duly rebuilt. However, the priory remained very poor.

The End of the Priory

After the Black Death, only four canons remained at the priory. The priory was fined 3s and 4d (the equivalent of almost £80 in modern terms) at the Augustinian Chapter in 1443 for not sending representatives to the chapter, and three years later the Northampton Chapter was informed that Berden had no more canons and had collapsed.

Prior Thomas Dane had trouble collecting his rents in the mid-fifteenth century; the tenants claimed that they'd paid John Ive of Rayleigh, the prior's receiver who'd recently died, and Ive's executors claimed that he'd paid every penny. Interestingly, Dane seemed to have similar problems in the Priory of Holy Trinity in London, as there's a memorandum of agreement from around 1439 saying that the prior should be given a pension, goods should be restored to the keeping of Thomas Dane, Dane and his supporters should not be molested, and Dane should have permission to leave the priory (presumably to go to Berden, as he appears there in 1441).

The priory was dissolved in 1536 and sold to Henry Parker, who sold it to Thomas Avery and his wife Margery.

Stone coffins that were dug up near the farmhouse are now in Saffron Walden museum.

❀ ❀ ❀

Bicknacre Priory

Bicknacre Priory (OS map reference TL78570268), near Woodham Ferrers, is the remains of an Augustinian priory dedicated to St Mary and St John the Baptist. The only remaining masonry is a single arch, which was the west arch of the crossing of the church, with attached fragments of the nave and the north transept. The arch is visible on Priory Field (NB the approach is quite muddy) but is kept behind a locked barrier.

The Beginning of the Priory

Originally there was a hermitage on the site occupied by man called Jordan. The priory was built on the site of the hermitage in 1175 by Maurice FitzGeoffrey of Tilty, the former sheriff of Essex, and there were 15 canons. It was known as Wodeham Priory until 1235, and then was called Bicknacre. In 1311 and 1313, the priory was sequestered by king because it couldn't meet its debts.

Remains of Bicknacre Priory; plate from Thomas Kitson Cromwell's
Excursions Through Essex, *1818-9.*

Dissolution and After

In 1507, prior Edmund Goding died. There were no canons at the priory so it was dissolved and the priory and its possessions (including the church, 30 houses, 300 acres of farmland, 40 acres of meadow, 44 acres of woodland and 500 acres of pasture in nearby villages) reverted to the king. The priory remained empty until 1509, when it was given to the Hospital of St Mary without Bishopsgate until Dissolution in 1536

In 1540 the site was granted to Henry Polsted of London. Part of the priory was demolished and the stone was used to repair local roads; part was converted into a house, which was repaired several times in the seventeenth and eighteenth centuries.

Arch at Priory Fields, Bicknacre.
Photograph by author.

According to Duffield William Coller, writing in 1861, some of the priory buildings were used as farmhouse back in 1812, but were later demolished. In 1832, the wall over the remaining arch was rebuilt and a pegtile roof was added; it's said that the bones of monks disturbed during the work were reinterred under the arch. The roof was restored again in 1997 and 2008.

In the early 1930s, wooden huts (known as 'holiday homes') were built in the field for children who went to Sunday school at church in Bethnal Green. They were closed at the start of the Second World War and the huts were used by local serviceman. After the war, the huts were used as storage by the department store Bonds of Chelmsford, and were later demolished.

The farm was sold in 2001 and Priory Fields – seven acres of land, including the remaining arch – was given to the parish council.

Spooks: the White Elm

According to tradition, the White Elm at Bicknacre grew from an elm stake that had been thrust through the heart of a highwayman who had been buried at the crossroads as a criminal.

❈ ❈ ❈

Blackmore Priory

Blackmore Priory (OS map reference TL855 222) was an Augustine monastery dedicated to St Laurence; it was founded by the de Sanford family near the end of the twelfth century. The only remains of the priory are two blocked thirteenth-century arches in the church of St Nicholas.

The Beginnings of the Priory

Richard, the Bishop of London, gave authorisation to build the priory in 1160. The land was given by Adam and Jordan de Sanford.

Scandals: Visitations

In 1309, the Bishop of London visited the priory; there were clearly problems because he left a long list of injunctions. The monks were told that they had to attend all services, 'cease from strife and contentions' among themselves, and not wander outside the precincts. They were also not to receive money for buying clothes. They were clearly also neglecting the parish church as they were told to put a priest there to say Mass and minister to the parishioners. They didn't do it, so on 14 Feb 1310 the bishop gave them 10 days to do it. Two months later, the prior and one of the canons appeared before the bishop and signed an agreement with five Blackmore parishioners that they would provide a parish vicar – and the penalty for not doing so was 40 shillings (the equivalent of just over £600 in modern terms).

There were more problems in 1446, when the Northampton Chapter was told that two of the canons of Blackmore had become apostate. There were two forms of apostasy in England: for a lay person, apostasy meant renouncing your faith, but if you were a professed religious person, apostasy meant leaving the religious life for a secular one without permission. In this case, it was probably the latter.

The End of the Priory

The priory was dissolved in 1525 by John Alen; originally, the revenues were going to be used to set up Cardinal Wolsey's college in Ipswich. In 1526 Wolsey granted the funds from the priory to his college at Oxford, and in 1529 transferred the funds to his college at Ipswich; then he fell from favour, and Henry VIII confiscated the priory. Eventually, Henry gave the land and buildings to John Smyth, one of his auditors. Smyth started pulling down the church so that he could build his house, Smyth's Hall; the villagers were furious and got an injunction to stop him, but they were too late as he'd already removed most of the building. All they could make him do was to brick up the east wall.

Henry VIII and Jericho

According to Rev. Philip Morant, writing in 1768:

> *The priory is reported to have been one of King Henry the VIII's Houses of Pleasure and was disguised by the name of Jericho, so that when this lascivious Prince had a mind to be lost in the embraces of his courtesans, the cant word among his courtiers, was that he was 'gone to Jericho'.*

It's pretty unlikely that Henry actually had trysts with his mistresses there, as he had ample opportunity for his affairs at court. However, it's known that he sent one of his favourite mistresses, Elizabeth Blount, to the priory at Blackmore. Elizabeth was a maid to Katherine of Aragon, and became Henry's mistress in 1518. When royal mistresses became pregnant, they were usually sent out of the public eye for a while; and on 18 June 1519 Elizabeth gave birth to Henry's son, Henry Fitzroy, at Blackmore. Henry VIII made him the Earl of Nottingham and Duke of Richmond and Somerset on 18 June 1525, and also made him knight of the garter.

Henry Fitzroy died aged 17 and was buried in the priory at Thetford in Norfolk.

The house behind the wall next to the church is still called Jericho; Pevsner says that it's a rebuilt house dating from 1714, when the original building was sold to shipbuilder Jacob Acworth. Acworth pulled the house down and discovered many bones and a lead coffin while digging the garden; clearly the land had once been the priory cemetery.

Jericho, Blackmore. Photograph by author.

Castle Hedingham Castle

Castle Hedingham Castle (OS map reference TL787358) is the Norman stone keep of a ringwork and bailey castle; the remains are around 35 metres high and are faced with ashlar masonry. It's rare for Norman castles to be completely faced with stone, but the de Vere family was rich and powerful enough to afford the cost of transporting the stone from quarries in Barnack. (It cost around £2,500 to build – at a time when the annual royal income was £10,000.)

Remains of Castle Hedingham castle; plate from Thomas Kitson Cromwell's Excursions Through Essex, *1818-9.*

The castle is privately owned and is open to the public in the summer. The architectural historian Nikolaus Pevsner calls it the 'best-preserved of all tower-keeps of England'; the walls are 12 feet thick at the base and 10 feet thick at the top.

The Beginnings of the Castle

According to the seventeenth-century historian Philip Morant, before the Norman Conquest the land belonged to the thane Ulfwine. William I gave the land to one of his knights, Alberic de Vere, who built a timber castle on the site; he also founded the priory of Earl's Colne – see page 60 – and is said to have laid out four new vineyards in England, including one at Hedingham.

Historians aren't sure who built the castle in stone; the two main candidates are Alberic's son, Aubrey de Vere II (who became Henry I's master chamberlain of England), and Aubrey II's son, Aubrey de Vere III (who became the first Earl of Oxford). The building work began some time between 1130 and 1140, and it's thought that the castle was designed by William de Corbeuil, the archbishop of Canterbury, as it's similar to his design at Rochester Castle.

Although the hall looks as if it has five storeys, it only has two; the upper windows were made to give extra light. The ground floor was used for storing provisions, and the garrison was housed on the first floor. There is also a minstrel's gallery running round the Great Hall, and a spiral staircase that was originally stone but was replaced in brick in the sixteenth century. There are Roman tiles in the fireplace, and the castle also contains the largest Norman arch in Europe (28 feet wide and 20 feet high).

The thirteenth Earl of Oxford rebuilt the castle in 1496 as a Tudor palace,

The mighty keep at Castle Hedingham.
Photograph by author.

including a 'donjon' that overlooked the town of Castle Hedingham, but the only survival of his work is the bridge spanning the moat. There are foundations for the stair turrets of the dungeon. Excavations in 1868 showed that the great hall was south west of the keep and the chapel was to the south.

Sieges: King John and the Rebel Barons

Aubrey de Vere III, the first Earl of Oxford, had to surrender his castles to Stephen in 1143 because he'd supported Matilda; however, he recovered Castle Hedingham later in the decade. Maud, Stephen's wife, died at Castle Hedingham on 3 May 1151 and was buried in Feversham Abbey.

The castle was besieged twice, in 1216 and 1217; both were relatively short sieges, and were won by those attacking the castle. Robert de Vere, the third Earl of Oxford, was present at Runnymede and was one of the 26 barons who made King John sign the Magna Carta on 15 June 1215. He was excommunicated when the Pope took John's side, and in 1216 de Vere joined the rebel barons in inviting the Dauphin of France to take the throne. Before the Dauphin was able to land, John besieged Colchester Castle and the French garrison surrendered to him; following his victory, the king marched to Hedingham and besieged the castle. De Vere's retainers threw fresh fish from the battlements of the keep in an attempt to convince John that they had plenty of food, so it was pointless for him to besiege them – but eventually they were forced to surrender and John declared the castle and lands forfeit to him.

Castle Hedingham.
Photograph by author.

The following year, the Dauphin besieged the castle and took it; but after John's death Henry III made peace with the barons, and de Vere's castle and lands were returned to him.

Never Try to Outwit a King…

Henry VII stayed at the castle in August 1498; John de Vere was one of Henry's favourites, as he was one of the main people who'd helped him gain the crown. Henry had a good stay and feasted well but, as he was leaving, de Vere's servants formed a line through which the king could pass – and they were all dressed in very fine livery with the de Vere arms prominently on display. The king rebuked de Vere for having so many 'menial servants' dressed so finely; although de Vere argued that he'd done it for the honour of the king, the king was well aware of the recent turbulence in the country and didn't want any nobleman becoming too powerful and threatening his position. He'd just passed a law forbidding his nobles from putting his retainers in livery. 'By my faith, my lord, I thank you for your good cheer, but I may not endure to have my laws broken in my sight,' he said – and fined his host 15,000 marks (the equivalent of around £5 million in modern terms)!

The de Vere Star

Aubrey de Vere II took part in the First Crusade to the Holy Land in 1098. At Antioch, his troops fought against the commander of the Sultan of Persia's forces; as darkness was falling, the Saracens thought they would be saved, but then a five-pointed star suddenly appeared on de Vere's standard and lit up the battlefield. The Crusaders won the battle, and the de Veres chose the five-pointed star as their emblem from then on.

The End of the Castle

By the early seventeenth century, most of the buildings had been lost, and the castle was no longer the seat of the Earls of Oxford. In 1713 the land was sold to Sir William Ashurst, Lord Mayor of London; he built a manor house there and landscaped its grounds but, according to Pevsner, Horace Walpole called it 'a trumpery new house… in the bad taste of architecture'.

Castle Hedingham Priory

Castle Hedingham Priory (OS map reference TL7779 3556) is the remains of a Benedictine nunnery. There's only a tiny masonry fragment left on the site, now occupied by Nunnery Farm; it originally stood around 750 yards west of the church (which Pevsner highlights as a complete Late Norman parish church with a rare Norman wheel window).

The Beginnings of the Priory

The priory was founded some time before 1191 by Aubrey de Vere (the first Earl of Oxford) and his wife, Agnes. It was dedicated to St Mary, St James and the Holy Cross, and originally had space for five nuns.

Scandals: Betrothal and Divorce

Probably one of the most notorious stories about Agnes and Aubrey took place long before the priory was even built. Agnes d'Essex was betrothed to Geoffrey de Vere at the age of three and was brought up in the de Vere household. However, she rejected the match with Geoffrey and instead became the third wife of his brother Aubrey, around 1161.

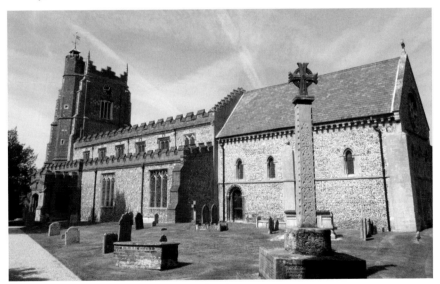

Castle Hedingham church. Photograph by author.

However, in 1163, Agnes' father Henry was involved in a huge scandal (see Rayleigh, page 102); he was disgraced and had to forfeit his lands and offices. The de Veres were horrified at the idea of being tarnished by the scandal, and tried to obtain a divorce for Aubrey – but Agnes refused to let them cast her off and took the case to court. On 9 May 1166, she appealed to the pope from the court of the Bishop of London (Thomas Becket, the Archbishop of Canterbury, was in exile at the time so she couldn't appeal through him).

In the meantime, Aubrey had Agnes confined to one of his castles, and the Bishop of London reprimanded him for it. The de Veres said that because Agnes was betrothed to Geoffrey, her marriage to Aubrey was invalid; the pope pointed out that because she'd been raised by the de Veres from the age of three, she hadn't had the chance to consent to or reject the plans. Before her twelfth birthday, Agnes had actually written to her father rejecting Geoffrey (in those days an unusual step), so the pope said her letter was enough to break her betrothal and leave her free to marry Aubrey. The case was used to develop the canon law of marriage, and from then on women were required to give their consent to betrothal and marriage.

The marriage was clearly successful after that, because Agnes and Aubrey had at least four sons and a daughter together, as well as establishing the nunnery. Four years after Aubrey's death in 1194, Agnes offered the king 100 marks for the right to marry whoever she wished – and remained unmarried until her death circa 1206, when she was buried next to her husband at Earls Colne.

Fire

The priory was burned down in 1190 by Aubrey, Agnes and Aubrey's son. The king fined him 100 marks and made him give extra property to the nunnery in reparation for his actions.

An Unwanted Nun

In 1279, Archbishop Peckham ordered the prioress and convent to admit Agnes, the daughter of Sir Roger Beauchamp, as a nun. When they refused, he wrote to them, threatening to punish them so severely that other nunneries wouldn't dare defy him again. He also pointed out that they would be wise to take Agnes as the queen was very fond of her (hinting that the queen would then be a benefactress to them).

The End of the Priory

The nunnery was dissolved in 1536 and the prioress, Mary Baynbrigge, was given a pension of 100 shillings a year. The priory site was granted to John de Vere, and the buildings were demolished. During the 1980s, a barn was built on Nunnery Street and during the work a number of skeletons were found.

The south door (aka 'skin door') at St Nicholas' church, Castle Hedingham. Photograph by author.

Spooks: the Skin Door

The south door at St Nicholas' church, Castle Hedingham, is also known as the 'skin door'. According to tradition, if a church robber was caught, his skin would be nailed to the door to deter any other would-be thieves. When the door was renovated in the nineteenth century, strips of what looked like leather or human skin were found beneath the ironwork.

Similar legends have been told about the churches in Hadstock and Copford, where the skin fragments allegedly belonged to Danes who tried to sack the church; the story at Hedingham is that 'a foreign robber' tried to sack the church. However, the Hadstock fragments were subject to DNA tests by the University of Oxford, which proved that the leather was the skin of a cow – Saxon church doors were often covered with leather to help keep out the draughts. As the fragments from Hedingham disappeared and weren't ever tested, we can only assume that the story – like the ones at Hadstock and Copford – was used to scare would-be robbers.

Scandal: the Hedingham Witchcraft Case

In March 1864, a nasty case was reported in the *Bury and Norwich Post*, where a mob decided to 'swim' an old man known as 'Dummy', to see if he was a wizard. One of the workhouse guardians brought the case against a local carpenter and a beerhouse-keeper's wife, accusing them of murdering the old man.

Dummy was believed to be around 80 years old; nobody actually knew his name or where he was born, though everyone believed that he was French. He'd lived near Sible Hedingham for the previous eight years and, although he was deaf and dumb, he was able to make himself understood by gestures. Apparently, he made his livelihood by telling fortunes.

He was definitely eccentric; he had a habit of wearing two or three coats and two or three hats at the same time, and was usually accompanied by three or four small dogs whenever he went on his travels.

Several times, Dummy visited Ridgewell, near Hedingham, and on one trip he wanted to sleep at the beerhouse belonging to Emma Smith's husband. Emma refused to let him stay, and Dummy made threatening signs and stroked his stick.

Shortly afterwards she fell ill and decided that he must have bewitched her. She begged him to remove the spell from her; when nothing happened, she met him at the Swan pub near Sible Hedingham on 3 August 1863. She offered him three sovereigns to come and sleep at the beerhouse in Ridgewell, but Dummy was terrified that if he went there he'd be hurt – so he refused, drawing three fingers across his throat.

Meanwhile, villagers who had heard rumours came to the Swan to find out what was going on, and a riot started. Emma Smith still wanted Dummy to go home with her; he refused, and she went crazy, beating him with a stick, kicking him and tearing his coat. She dragged him down to the nearby brook, saying, 'You old devil, you served me out – now I will serve you out,' and pushed him in to the water. When Dummy tried to get out, the carpenter, Mr Stammers, came to her aid and pushed him back. Dummy finally managed to get out, but Smith and Stammers dragged him back into the brook and pushed him in to the deepest part. Someone called out that if they didn't get the old man out, he'd die, so Stammers pulled him out of the water. They took him to the miserable hut where he lived, and he spent the night there in wet, muddy clothes. The next day, Mr Fowke, the workhouse guardian, came to see Dummy and discovered him still wet, trembling and badly bruised. He reported the case to the local constable and had Dummy taken to the workhouse at Halstead, where he was treated by the surgeon, but died a month later.

The surgeon said that he believed Dummy had died 'from disease of the kidneys produced by immersion in water and sleeping in wet clothes'. The jury found Stammers and Smith guilty and sentenced them both to six months' hard labour.

✤ ✤ ✤

Chich Abbey, St Osyth's

Chich Abbey (OS map reference TM122 157) is also known as St Osyth's Priory, and was the third largest monastery in Essex after Barking and Waltham. However, the site of the original nunnery is traditionally placed in Nun's Wood, about 1km north-west of the village (OS map reference TM116 166).

The Legend of St Osyth

The original nunnery was founded by St Osyth, who was the daughter of Frithwald (the first Christian king of the East Saxons) and Wilburga (the daughter of the king of Mercia). Miracles were ascribed to her right from her early life. As a young girl, she was sent by King Alfred's sister Edith to Warwickshire, to take a book to St Modwen, but was blown off a bridge by a gust of wind and drowned in the river. Edith was worried when the girl didn't return and followed in her footsteps; St Modwen met her at the bridge and said that an angel had directed her to the river. Modwen and Edith spoke to some shepherds, who said that they'd seen her by the bridge; they prayed together, called her name three times, and she reappeared out of the river, restored to life.

The eighteenth-century historian Philip Morant says that St Osyth was born in Quarenden, Aylesbury, and was brought up by her aunt in Elesborough in the Chilterns.

Osyth was betrothed to Sighere, the king of Essex; according to Morant, she had made a vow of virginity but her father forced her into the marriage. At the wedding, a white hart ran past and Sighere and his courtiers chased after it. Osyth seized her chance and ran off to a nunnery. Sighere, realising that this was her true vocation and that she didn't want to be married to him, gave her his manor of Cicc (Chich) and she built a nunnery there, dedicated to the Holy Trinity.

In October 653, the Danes ravaged the area; Morant says that they were led by Ingmar and Hubba. When Osyth refused to worship their gods, they cut off her head. Osyth then took her head in her hands and walked to the

Remains of Chich Abbey gateway; plate from Thomas Kitson Cromwell's Excursions Through Essex, *1818-9.*

31

church of St Peter and St Paul; the door was closed, so she struck it with her hand and then fell down. A spring gushed forth (still visible in Nun's Wood) which had the reputation of curing diseases, particularly impotency; the spring was later piped by the monks.

Although Osyth was buried at Chich, her parents decided to take her body to Aylesbury; 46 years later, her body miraculously reappeared back in Chich.

Remains of Chich Abbey;
plate from Thomas Kitson Cromwell's
Excursions Through Essex, *1818-9.*

Apparently miracles were wrought at her tomb in Chich and also at Aylesbury. And when Alfword, the Bishop of London, tried to steal her bones in 1044, he was struck down with leprosy – a warning not to mess with the saint.

St Osyth Priory gateway. Photograph by author.

The Beginning of the Monastery

In 1121, an Augustinian priory was founded at St Osyth's by Richard de Belmeis, the bishop of London. Apparently he'd taken some of the lands to make a park; when he suffered a stroke, he believed that it was as a result of St Osyth being angry with him for his actions, so on his recovery he founded the priory. It became an abbey in 1150, and was dedicated to Saints Peter and Paul and St Osyth.

There was an earthquake in 1381, which brought down some of the sea wall and the sea flowed in to the abbey lands as far as the sacristy.

Stained glass window showing the martyrdom of St Osyth in the church of St Peter and St Paul, St Osyth.
Photograph by author.

Scandals: Visitations, Thieves & Prisoners

The abbey had disciplinary problems from at least the beginning of the fourteenth century. There was a visitation in 1304 by the Archbishop of Canterbury, who said that there should be 30 canons but fewer than 20 were actually at the abbey. Clearly discipline was a real problem, because they were told that they had to keep all the offices, and when they were allowed to talk it had to be about religion instead of 'unworthy gossip'. They also weren't not allowed out alone, and women were absolutely not allowed in the bakehouse. Worldliness also seemed to be creeping in, because the monks were told that they all had to wear the same colour and sort of garments. The abbot and canons were also rebuked for entertaining their friends in town – under the rules of their order, this wasn't allowed, even if the 'friend' was royalty!

In 1306, the abbot stole a cross from the hospital of Dunwich in Suffolk. The monks at Dunwich complained that they had fewer visitors who gave alms because of the loss of the cross; they took him to court and he had to give it back. Two years later, John de Walden, one of the canons from Royston, was sent to St Osyth for three years' imprisonment and penance; on Wednesdays and Fridays, he was only allowed to have bread and water. Royston had to pay St Osyth's 12d a week for his maintenance (the equivalent of £20 in modern terms) because, unless the monasteries exchanged monks, the priory sending the monk away had to pay for his maintenance in the place where he was kept. However, in January 1310 the bishop sent him back to Royston. Also in 1308, Robert de Stratford, a canon of St Osyth's, was sent to St Bartholomew's in Smithfield; St Osyth's had to pay St Bartholomew's 1s a week for his keep. Under the terms of his penance, he was only allowed to have bread, soup and beer on Mondays and Wednesdays, and nothing but bread and water on Fridays. He also had to attend all the canonical services, celebrate Mass daily and take the last place in choir and in the refectory; he was not allowed to leave the enclosure or meet women (which gives a clue, perhaps, to his misdemeanours). Sadly for Robert, his penance was indefinite.

When Bishop Baldock visited St Osyth's in 1308, things clearly hadn't improved from the last visitation because he gave exactly the same injunctions; he added that the canons were not allowed to give money to their relatives for clothes and shoes.

In 1310, there was a fight in Royston priory, when canon Walter de Kelishulle drew his sword against the prior and much blood was spilled in the church. The bishop gave him leave to go to Rome for absolution, and on his return he was sent to St Osyth's. The terms of his penance were that he was to be last in the refectory, church and dormitory; on Wednesdays and Fridays, he was only allowed to have bread, cheese and pottage; and Royston had to pay 14d a week for his keep.

St Osyth's was clearly becoming a place for imprisonment, because in 1325 the king sent Laurence de Tonbrigg there from the tower of London. De Tonbrigg was accused of being an apostate (i.e. leaving the religious life for a secular one without permission). He wasn't allowed to leave the cloister/church and he wasn't allowed to speak to any 'suspicious person'. Other apostates at St Osyth included canon John de Thaxstede, who was ordered to be readmitted in 1345 (he'd left four years before to join the Friars Minor and had said that he would never come back), and John Stury, in 1391, who was ordered to be sent to the abbot for punishment for being an apostate and vagabond canon.

In 1433 Dr Zanobius Mulakyn gave a truly bad report at the visitation. He said that Abbot Fowler had sold the lead utensils of the larder 'for voluptuous purposes' and accounts were not made up properly. He also accused the abbot of using chalices for 'profane' things, stealing offerings that had been made to the shrine of St Osyth, and drinking too much. The abbot admitted his guilt and promised to mend his ways – but he didn't, and eventually the bishop said that he was 'contumacious and an evil administrator' and suspended him. His punishment included deprivation (which meant that he'd get no pension), but the abbot begged the bishop personally for forgiveness and asked if he could resign instead and keep enough pension to live on. The problems didn't stop there, though; the bishop elected John Depyng (the prior of St Botolph's in Colchester) as the abbot. Depyng asked permission of St Botolph's to take goods and money owing from debtors to refurnish Chich; he said that he'd repay it quickly, but then didn't pay anything at all. When he died, the monks of St Botoph asked the new abbot, William Kent, to repay the debt; he refused, so they were forced to take him to court (though the result of the case is unknown).

One really unusual case occurred in 1452. John Wynton was originally from St Osyth's; the pope gave him dispensation to become a beneficed priest. According to historian F. Donald Logan, Wynton might be the earliest monk in England who was allowed to wear secular clothes (provided that he wore his religious habit underneath).

Thomas Bledlow of Dunstable Priory had become an apostate three times during his career (once for twenty years) and was called a notorious murderer and adulterer. In 1446, at the age of eighty, he appealed to be readmitted to Dunstable – but he was clearly quite a hardened character as the monks were too frightened of him to let him come back, and he was sent to St Osyth's instead.

Scandal: Conspiracy Against the King

Abbot Thomas de London joined the Abbot of Colchester in 1403 in the conspiracy against Henry IV for Richard II to be restored to the throne (see also Beeleigh on page 15, and Colchester on page 44 for the full story). There was an order for his arrest in 1404, but he was eventually pardoned and his goods were returned.

The End of the Abbey

Thomas Legh visited St Osyth's in 1535 and advised Thomas Solmes, one of the monks, to write a letter to Cromwell. Solmes asked for licence to leave and said that he only joined the monastery because his schoolteacher threatened him to make him do it; he became a monk before he was 14, had been there for 12 years and hated it, and said would rather die than have to keep living such a miserable life. He wasn't on the list of monks who surrendered, so presumably Cromwell agreed.

Thomas Audeley asked for St Osyth's to be made secular college, but Cromwell ordered its dissolution; it was finally dissolved on 28 July 1539. The riches included 'the skull of Seynt Osithes closyed in sylver parcel gylte' and 'a croune of sylver gylte too sett apon the sayd skull garnysshyd with counterfett stones'. The lead on the roofs was worth £1,044 (an astonishing £449,000 in modern terms).

There were clearly plenty of servants at the abbey; among the servants listed in the inventory were valetti (general servants), pandoxatores (who worked in the brewhouse and bakehouse), coqui (cooks), bigami (waggoners), pueri (acolytes) and lavenders (laundresses). The local goldsmith and his servant were also given rewards for 'waying of the Platte & for defassing of the shryne'.

Cromwell took a fancy to the place and it was granted to him. From him, it passed to Lord Darcy, Earl Rivers, who demolished the abbey church and some of the buildings in 1553, and converted some of the rest into a house. After Darcy's death, the abbey fell into decay, but eventually the Earl of Rochford moved in. In 1768 he brought some poplar trees from Lombardy and had them planted in the park; they were thought to be the first poplar trees planted in England. The house was remodelled again in 1865.

Spooks

On 7 October, it's said that St Osyth appears, carrying her head. In the 1970s, a monk was seen walking around the buildings at night, carrying a candle, and when the abbey became a nursing home, several residents said they saw monks walking by a window. During the 1990s, a middle-aged woman wearing a flowery hat suddenly appeared in the back seat of a car; when the driver pulled over, shaken, the passenger disappeared.

Spooks: Dragons

Perhaps the strangest story about the abbey dates from 9 March 1170, when it's said that a dragon attacked the house; the chronicler Ralph Niger said that the dragon was 'of marvellous bigness', and the legend was repeated in a broadsheet of 1704. Apparently the air around the dragon was so hot that the area was set alight. Another legend says that the dragon had its lair in the cellars of the abbey. There is a beautiful dragon carved in the spandrels of the gateway to the abbey.

Spooks: The Witches of St Osyth

Ursula Kempe was a local midwife who had a reputation for removing spells. Allegedly, she curved Davy Thorlowe of illness, but when Davy's mother Grace refused to employ Ursula as a nursemaid for her daughter Joan, Ursula was furious. The little girl fell out of her cot and broke her neck, and everyone suspected that Ursula was to blame. Despite this, when Grace suffered from arthritis, she asked Ursula for treatment; but then she refused to pay the treatment fee of a shilling, and her condition worsened. Grace went to the magistrates and claimed that Ursula was a witch.

At the trial, the magistrate, Bryan Darcy (who also happened to be Thorlowe's employer) offered clemency if she'd admit her guilt. So Ursula testified that she had four familiars – two cats, called Tytty and Jacke; a toad called Pygine, and a lamb called Tyffin – which she fed on cake, beer and her own blood. According to her, Jack killed her sister-in-law, and Tyffin killed baby Thorlowe. She then went on to name four other women as witches: Alice Hunt, Alice Newman, Elizabeth Bennet and Margery Sammon, who in turn confessed and named another nine witches.

At the end of the trial, two of the women were not indicted as witches; four were acquitted; two were discharged but kept in prison for other offences; four were found guilty and reprieved; and Ursula Kempe and Elizabeth Bennet were hanged in Chelmsford in 1582.

In 1921, two skeletons were discovered in a garden in St Osyth by Mr Charles Brooker. They had iron rivets in their knees and elbows, and were thought to be Kempe and Bennet – although historian Dr Alison Rowlands has challenged this, as the bones haven't been tested or dated.

Clavering Castle

Clavering Castle (OS map reference TL 471 320) is the remains of a Norman castle with pre-Norman ringwork and earthworks. There are only about 200 ringwork castles in the country, and only 60 of them have baileys. The earthworks are situated north of church of St Mary and St Clement, and its moat is 75 feet wide and 18 feet deep.

The Beginnings of the Castle

The original settlement at Clavering was pre-Norman, but the first known Lord of Clavering was Robert Fitz Wymarc, who was one of Edward the Confessor's closest aides. Fitz Wymarc was a Norman knight who was related to William of Normandy (later William the Conqueror) and had lived in England for many years; he was known as the king's staller (i.e. master of his horses). He was also the king's standard-bearer and was

Moat at Clavering castle, behind the church.
Photograph by author.

the sheriff of both Essex and Hertfordshire. He had large landholdings in Essex and is one of the four people shown on the Bayeux Tapestry next to Edward's head as the king lies dying.

'Robert's Castle', mentioned in the Domesday survey, is thought to be Clavering, though some sources associate it with the castle at Great Canfield (see page 62).

The castle was built somewhere between 1048 and 1052; a survey in 1977 showed foundations of buildings under the surface, but there isn't a motte and it's probable that the castle buildings were made of wood.

In 1052, according to the *Anglo-Saxon Chronicle*, some of the French party at Edward the Confessor's court sheltered at the castle at Clavering on their way back to France.

When William the Conqueror landed at Pevensey in 1066, Fitz Wymarc tried to persuade him not to fight Harold – he said that William didn't have the strength or the numbers to defeat Harold. William proved him wrong, but held no grudge

Earthworks at Clavering castle, behind the church. Photograph by author.

against Fitz Wymarc and let him keep his lands. Fitz Wymarc lived at Clavering until his death, when his son Sweyn inherited the castle; however, Sweyn settled at Rayleigh rather than Clavering (see page 102).

The End of the Castle

It's not known how the castle met its end; it's possible that the end came during the civil war between Stephen and Matilda, or it might have been destroyed by King John after 1215. It was certainly abandoned by the end of the thirteenth century.

Discovery

When workmen were putting up a fence round the churchyard in 1923, they discovered a slab of stone. Further investigation showed that it was the lid of a coffin. It was seven feet long and two feet wide with walls six inches thick, and weighed a ton. It contained what contemporary reports called 'a well-preserved skeleton of a man… the skull was that of an intellectual head, and the teeth were perfect'. The site of the discovery was on the edge of the castle moat, and it's thought that a chapel had once been built there. The body was reinterred.

Coggeshall Abbey

Coggeshall Abbey (OS map reference TL855 222) is the remains of a Savigniac (later Cistercian) monastery dedicated to St John.

The History of the Abbey

According to a chronicle from the abbey, Coggeshall Abbey was founded by King Stephen and Queen Maud in 1142. The Savigniac order collapsed in 1147, and by the time the church was built in 1167 the monastery was fully part of the Cistercian order. The monastery was then dedicated to St Mary. Most of the remains are simply foundations, but there are some remains of cloister which are now part of Abbey Farm, and the house contains part of the infirmary. It is on private land and is not open to the public.

Remains of Coggeshall Abbey; plate from Thomas Kitson Cromwell's Excursions Through Essex, *1818-9.*

St Nicholas' chapel was built in the thirteenth century as the gatehouse chapel; sadly, it is kept locked, although it can be viewed from the outside. The monks at Coggeshall were brickmakers, and the bricks in the abbey and the gatehouse chapel are thought to be oldest post-Roman bricks in the country.

The abbey was dissolved in 1538. The church became a barn, then in 1863 was restored as the parish church.

Spooks: Ghostly Monks

A monk with pale face and lighted taper is said to walk round the abbey, then head down the lane to the Blackwater River. Other monks are said to have once held secret meetings in Cradle House; so the story goes, they come back and dance in the garden.

Spooks: Robin the Woodcutter

Robin the Woodcutter was a local tradesman and woodcarver; his ghost has been seen since the 1600s near the brook, and people have claimed to hear the sound of

St Nicholas' chapel – remains of Coggeshall Abbey.
Photograph by author.

his axe and whistling in the woods. He is said to have carved a beautiful image called the 'Angel of the Christmas Mysteries'. The statue was hidden during the Reformation and never found afterwards.

Ralph, the Sixth Abbot

One of the most famous monks from Coggeshall was Ralph, the sixth abbot, who was also a historian. He was present at the fall of Jerusalem to the Saracens in 1187, and sustained a bad head wound in the siege. He wrote the chronicle of the Holy Land; the last entry was in 1191, when he returned to England and settled at Coggeshall Abbey. He became abbot in 1207 but retired due to illness; he lived at Coggeshall for another ten years.

Scandal: Looted by King John

According to Ralph the historian, on the day of the Circumcision, 1216, while tierce (the third of the canonical services of the day) was being said, some of King John's army violently entered the abbey and carried off twenty-two horses of the bishop of London and others.

Scandal: the Vanishing Templars

During the time of the fourth abbot (Peter, 1176-94), Robert, the lay brother who was meant to care for guests, went into the refectory, where he discovered several people dressed like Templars. He talked to them, then went to tell the abbot about the visitors; but when he returned they'd gone and the porter claimed they'd never come through the gates.

Scandal: Investigations and Revolts

In 1370, the abbey was investigated by the king's escheator when it claimed that it was poor. The investigation revealed that the poverty was caused by having to grant too many corrodies (i.e. an allowance of food and clothing from a religious house, usually to a royal servant, and lodging was often included), granting lands to others at too low a rent, and spending too much.

John de Haverhill, the prior of Coggeshall, had a warrant out for his arrest as an apostate in August 1380, following a dispute over who would be prior.

Clearly the abbey was not popular, because during the revolt of 1381 the rebels entered the abbey and took goods, charters, writings and muniments.

John Hollingbourne, who was originally from Robertsbridge Abbey in Sussex, was exiled to Coggeshall for 'carnal lapses'. He fled to Rome and was given absolution in 1403.

The End of the Abbey

In 1535, during Dr Legh's visitation, the monks made accusations against the abbot, William Love. They claimed that he'd told them to pretend not to know some of the silver plate existed so the king couldn't have it; that he let lands at well below market value so the king couldn't have them; and that he refused to say a collect at high mass for the King and Queen. They also accused him of practising immorality and divination (apparently 'by means of a key and a book and a man's name').

The Earls of Essex and Oxford said that they'd examined they abbot and he was a true man; according to them, the accusations were made by 'a simple person' supported by the former abbot, Sampford, who had a grudge against Abbot Love. However, Essex and Oxford had both been stewards of the abbey, so it's unlikely that they would be impartial. It's possible that some of the accusations were trumped up by Abbot Sampford; but William Love was deprived of his post in 1536 and Henry More, the abbot of Tower Hill, was appointed to take over. More said almost straightaway that the porter spoke treasonable words, so perhaps there was some truth in Sampford's accusations. The abbey surrendered in February 1538, in debt.

Tunnels

Coggeshall Abbey is said to have a tunnel leading all the way to Colchester. Allegedly the tunnel went under the A120 and, during the time that horses were the main means of transport, it was possible to hear the change in tone of their hooves as waggons passed over the spot.

Colchester Abbey
(St John the Baptist)

Colchester Abbey (OS map reference TL9983 2468) is the remains of a Benedictine monastery dedicated to St John. The remains include the north gatehouse (which dates from the fifteenth century but had to be rebuilt in brick in the seventeenth century, as it was badly damaged during the siege of 1648) and part of the perimeter wall (which was excavated in 1971-2; it was a Norman wall that was refaced in probably the sixteenth century).

Gateway to St John's Abbey, Colchester.

The Beginnings of the Abbey

The abbey was founded by Eudo, the son of Hubert de Ria, towards the end of the eleventh century. Eudo was the Dapifer (or sewer) of William Rufus and lord of the town of Colchester. He chose to build the abbey on the site of a pre-Conquest church dedicated to St John the Baptist, where a priest called Siric served; there is also a Roman cemetery under the site.

Apparently Eudo chose the site because miracles had already been seen at the church – heavenly lights, plus voices heard when nobody was inside. But the miracle that really impressed Eudo was that of a man who was in fetters at the king's command. At the feast of St John, while Mass was being said, all the bolts flew out of the man's fetters and he was left free. Eudo took that as a sign that he should build the monastery on the site and dedicate it to St John.

Maurice, the bishop of London, was

Gateway to St John's Abbey, Colchester; plate from Thomas Kitson Cromwell's Excursions Through Essex, *1818-9.*

present when the building was marked out on 29 August 1096. Eudo laid the first stone of the abbey in 1097. The Bishop of Rochester sent two monks there, but they asked to return home and were replaced by two more. Eudo gave some tithes to the monks, but it cost as much to collect the taxes as they were actually worth, so there wasn't enough left for the monks to live on afterwards. Eventually, they gave up and left. Eudo thought about giving up the idea of having his abbey, but then he met with the Abbot of York, who sent 13 monks to help him. Eudo gave the monks more funds and building work continued. One of the monks, Hugh, became abbot.

The building was consecrated by the bishop of London in 1104; originally, the monks lived on the north side of the abbey, but they found it too noisy so they moved to the south side. Gradually, the number of monks grew to 20.

Miracle at Colchester

While Thomas Becket, the Archbishop of Canterbury, was in exile, a monk called Ralph came to the Abbey and was treated very kindly. He went back to Canterbury when Becket returned, and was there when the archbishop was murdered. Ralph collected some of Becket's blood in a glass vessel, sealed it with wax and sent it to Colchester as a gift of thanks for their kind treatment of him. He only sent them a couple of drops of blood, but they wrote back and said that the vessel was full and that blood was oozing through the wax. The abbot washed the wax and gave the water to a neighbouring church, but the water vanished by the next morning. Several members of the household were allegedly cured by the water in which the wax was washed.

The abbey burned down in 1133 and was rebuilt in a cruciform plan. Henry III gave the abbey 15 oaks towards the rebuilding costs in 1235.

Scandal: Fight Between Town and Gown

There was a row in 1253 when the abbot accused nearly 40 of the leading men of Colchester of cutting the ropes of his ships on the River Colne and dismantling his gallows. But there was a much bigger row in 1272, when there was a riot at the midsummer fair between the men of the town and the monks. The next day, the coroner was taken to see a dead man on St John's Field and was told that the townsmen had killed him. At the inquest, the coroner discovered that the monks had taken the thief from the town gallows and made out that he'd been murdered!

Scandal: Visitation

During the visitation of 1310, it was clear that discipline in the monastery was a problem. The bishop's injunctions said that the monks had to maintain the rule of silence, and meat was only to be given to the monks in the infirmary who were elderly or having medical treatment; plus they had to go through the proper channels to get clothes and shoes rather than going shopping.

Scandal: the French Prisoner who was Sold

In 1346, a Frenchman who called himself Berengar de Monte Alto and claimed that he was the Archdeacon of Paris was captured in France (probably at Crecy) by some of the English army. The soldiers then deserted and sold him in England for £50 (the equivalent of almost £25,000 in modern terms). He ended up in the hands of the abbot of Colchester – who promptly sold him and took him to London, despite the king's order that he should be detained. The abbot was consequently in hot water for disobeying the king!

Siege: St John versus St Botolph

In 1363, the abbot complained to the pope, saying that the canons of the nearby priory of St Botolph's had attacked the monk Thomas Stuckele and blockaded the abbey with 200 men. The abbot claimed that the men of St Botolph's had forced their way into the abbey and hurt him and his monks. The cause of the riot isn't clear, but may be linked to a dispute between the two houses over the church of St Peter.

Siege: the Uprising of 1381

John Ball, one of the leaders of the Uprising of 1381, had been the chaplain at St James' church in Colchester. During the Uprising, the Moot Hall was attacked; however, their manorial records survived. On 30 September, rioters attacked Moot Hall again and St John's Abbey; several court rolls from the abbey belonging to the manors of Greenstead and West Donyland were burned

Scandal: the Treasonous Abbot

Abbot Geoffrey Storey ended up in strife at the bishop's visitation, when the bishop found him negligent and said that his misgovernment of the abbey had caused waste and dilapidation. At first, the abbot submitted to the bishop's orders, but then he rebelled – he cut down on the food and clothing of the prior and the monks, and took the possessions of the house for himself. He was also accused of riding with twelve armed men and disturbing the public peace. The king ordered the abbot's arrest in December 1392 and took him to the Chancery court to settle the dispute.

Ten years later, the abbot ended up joining a conspiracy with the Countess of Oxford to restore Richard II to the throne. Geoffrey persuaded the abbot of Beeleigh to join him, saying that Richard was alive and would be arriving in England shortly, backed by the French. However, but Richard didn't arrive and the French didn't invade; the plot was quickly discovered. Warrants were issued for the arrest of the conspirators – including two monks at the abbey, Johyn Herst and William Denton. The abbot fled, and the abbey was put in the custody of the Archbishop of Canterbury and the Bishop of Lincoln,

The abbot was eventually pardoned by the queen, but his goods were seized. He was arrested again in 1405 for treason. As he was ill in bed with a bad throat, he was carried to Colchester town hall in a chair and imprisoned there for five weeks before being taken to the castle at Nottingham. He died shortly afterwards; his successor, Roger Best, was also charged with treason in 1409, but was pardoned.

Scandal: More Rows Between Town and Gown

In 1429-30, abbot Robert Gryttone was in strife with the townsfolk over the liberties of Greensted; he accused various people of Lollardy, as well as saying that the town owed him £228 (the equivalent of almost £100,000 in modern terms) because they hadn't paid the abbey 20s a year during the years 1199 to 1427, which they'd promised to do under an agreement with King Stephen. The town retaliated by charging him and his predecessors for 130 years for not celebrating mass three days a week in St Helen's Chapel, which the abbey had agreed to do under a judgement in 1290. Clearly the counter-claims cancelled each other out, because things seemed to settle down again for a while.

Scandal: the Lost Prince

Lecturer David Baldwin from the University of Leicester has a theory that one of the two princes in the tower might not have been murdered in 1483. After Edward IV died, his sons Edward and Richard, aged 12 and 9, were locked in the Tower of London and were never seen again. Richard III has been accused of killing them after Parliament declared them illegitimate and he was crowned king, but nobody knows what really happened. In 1674, two skeletons were found under the stairs at the Tower; although they were reburied in Westminster abbey, it hasn't been proved that the skeletons were those of the two princes.

David Baldwin believes that 12-year-old Edward died of natural causes and 9-year-old Richard was allowed to live with his mother Elizabeth Woodville under guard. David also believes that Richard was taken to St John's Abbey after the battle of Bosworth and worked there as a bricklayer until the Dissolution. He notes that bricklayer 'Richard Plantaganet' died at Eastwell in Kent in 1550. Unusually for a bricklayer, Richard could read Latin; he told his employers that he was Richard III's natural son, but Baldwin thinks he might actually have been Edward IV's legitimate son.

The End of the Abbey and the Executed Abbot

Colchester Abbey was the fourth largest monastic institution in Essex, so it escaped the first wave of the Dissolution. Abbot Thomas Marshall (aka Thomas Beche), the sub-prior John Frances and two older monks refused to take the oath of fealty. Thomas Tye (aka Thomas Essex) wrote to Cromwell, complaining that Frances made 'seditious and slanderous words against the king's highness and his most honourable council'. The abbot and sub-prior were taken to court and examined, and judged it politic to take the oath of supremacy.

When it became obvious that the larger monasteries would also be dissolved, the abbey gained the favour of the chancellor, Sir Thomas Audeley, through exchanges of lands. Audeley wrote to the king, asking him to turn the abbeys of Colchester and St Osyth's (Chich) into secular colleges. His excuse was that 'Seynt Johns stondyth in his graces owne towne at Colchester wherein dwell many poor people which have daily relefe of the house'. The king refused, and Cromwell ordered dissolution of the two abbeys.

But the abbot had been dining out and speaking a little too freely. He'd been accused of treasonous words and managed to get out of it by claiming that there were no witnesses and it was his word against that of William Hall; but then he actually said to Sir John Seyncler, 'The kyng shall never have my howse but agayne my will and agayne my hart, for I knowe by my lernyng that he cannot take yt by right and lawe.' Seyncler promptly wrote to Cromwell, adding, 'My lorde I lyke not the man. I fere he hath a cankred harte.'

The abbot was taken to the Tower of London and accused of treason. His servant and two friends gave evidence against him, including that he'd said, 'two or three of the king's council had brought his grace to such a covetous mind that if all the water in Thames did flow gold and silver it were not able to quench his grace's thirst.' The abbot also openly lamented the death of Sir Thomas More to the local physician, Thomas Nuthake, and said that the king had turned away from Rome and made himself the head of the church so he could be divorced and marry Anne.

Thomas Marshall was tried, found guilty of treason and hanged at Colchester on 1 December 1539. Sir Christopher Jenny, one of the commissioners at the trial, wrote to Cromwell saying that the abbot asked for forgiveness and 'showed himself to be very penitent' – except that he still said that the suppression of the monasteries was against the law of God. Because the abbot had been attainted of treason, the abbey and its possessions then belonged to the king. He granted pensions to the monks, and leased the site to Sir Thomas Darcy.

In 1648, the abbey belonged to the Lucas family and was used as a royalist outpost (see Colchester Castle on page 49). It was badly damaged during the siege, and the upper gatehouse was destroyed by the Parliamentarians when they stormed it. The abbey was used to house Dutch prisoners in the 1660s, and then demolished. The gatehouse was restored in the 1840s, and twenty years later was purchased by the war office. It has been restored twice since, in 1951 and 1984, and at the time of writing, spring 2010, the precinct wall is being repaired.

Colchester Castle

Colchester Castle (OS map reference TL 998 253) is a Norman stone keep and bailey fortress that was built on the foundations of the Roman Temple of Claudius (itself built in AD 44). It's the largest Norman keep in Europe, measuring 46m by 34m (152 feet by 112 feet). A barbican with round flanking turrets was added in the thirteenth century. The castle is in the care of Colchester Museums and is open to the public daily.

The Beginnings of the Castle

William the Conqueror ordered his steward, Eudo Dapifer, to build the castle in stone. Eudo supervised the beginning of the construction, possibly from around 1070 and 1076. Building had to stop in 1075-6 – possibly because resources were diverted to head off the East Anglian rebellion based at Norwich, where Ralph de Guader and the Earl of Hereford planned to drive William out of the country and divide the land between them and the Earl of Northumberland, with one ruling as king and

Right: Eudo Dapifer, first ruler of Colchester Castle – monument on Colchester Town Hall.

Colchester Castle.

47

the other two remaining as earls – but the castle was finished by about 1101 and Eudo held the castle until his death in 1120, when it reverted to the Crown. Roman bricks and clay were used to build it, and holes for scaffolding poles can still be seen in the building. The original castle had perhaps three storeys; two still remain.

Sieges: King John

Surprisingly, the castle wasn't involved in the civil war between Stephen and Matilda; however, it suffered under the reign of King John. The castle walls were strengthened in 1214-15; although John came to Colchester, hoping to win over the constable of the castle, William de Lanvalai, he failed – de Lanvalai joined the rebel barons at Bury St Edmunds. John sent Stephen Harengood, one of his Flemish mercenaries, to take over the castle; however, when John signed the Magna

Two views showing the Exterior and Interior of Colchester Castle; plate from Thomas Kitson Cromwell's Excursions Through Essex, *1818-9.*

Carta, Harengood had to surrender the castle. The barons promptly put a French garrison into the castle in 1215.

During the Civil War, John besieged the castle for three months, then sent in the mercenary Savory de Meulon to win it back for him. The French soldiers inside – 115 of them – were allowed to leave for London; but, although they'd expected to be allowed to go to France, instead they were arrested in London. The English among the garrison were held to ransom.

In 1217, the French reoccupied the castle for Louis Dauphin, but the castle reverted back to royal hands.

The Castle as Prison

The castle was first recorded as a gaol in 1226; the criminals kept there were accused of theft, murder, treason and piracy. Henry III ordered Jews to be held at the castle in 1253.

The castle was used as the county prison from the fourteenth century, and Sir Thomas Malory – author of the *Morte d'Arthur* – was imprisoned there during the Wars of the Roses in 1454. He made a dramatic armed breakout from the castle, using swords, daggers and *'langues-de-boeuf'* (a kind of halberd), but was recaptured and returned to prison in London. Matthew Hopkins interrogated suspected witches there in 1645; and, although the castle was no longer the county gaol after 1668, it was still used as a prison until 1835.

Siege: the Royalist Rebels

During the Civil War, Colchester backed Parliament against the king and provided troops and horses. In 1642, Sir John Lucas was suspected of gathering arms for the king, and a mob looted his house at St John's Abbey and smashed his family's tombs in St Giles' church.

Charles I surrendered on 5 May 1646, but still had support in some parts of the country. When the Mayor of Canterbury tried to ban Christmas in 1647, the Royalists used it as an excuse to stir up rebellion. In May 1648, Lord Goring raised a Royalist army in Kent and was joined by Sir Charles Lucas (Sir John's brother) and Sir George Lisle. They failed to capture London, so they moved into Essex, heading for Norfolk. On 12 June 1648, the army of 4,000 arrived at Colchester and demanded to be let in. The townsfolk thought it would only be for a couple of days and reluctantly agreed – the mayor threw the keys over the wall so he wouldn't have to open the gate – but then Sir Thomas Fairfax and the Parliamentarian army arrived and demanded that the town should surrender.

Lucas and Lisle refused, and Fairfax besieged Colchester for twelve weeks. Nobody was allowed in or out, food became scarce, and the army bombarded the town wall and houses. People were forced to eat dogs and cats, rats – and even, incredibly, candles.

In August 1648, Lucas and Lisle could see how desperate the situation was; people were starving, sick or wounded. Townspeople begged Goring to surrender, but he refused. Meanwhile, women and children lay outside his house, 'howling and crying on the ground for bread'. Lucas demanded that the townsfolk should be given grain from the Royalists' stores, but it didn't last long and some went out to the Parliamentarian army and begged them for help – but Colonel Rainsborough refused and made them return to the town. Fairfax wouldn't let the starving people leave the town because he wanted to keep the pressure up.

Monument to Charles Lucas and George Lisle in the castle grounds, Colchester.

Finally, on 27 August, Colonel Tuke was sent by the Royalists to receive terms for surrender. Meanwhile the Parliamentarian army shot the sick members of the Royalist army and sent the healthy ones to prison or to the West Indies as slaves (despite saying they would give the solders 'fair quarter') – and Fairfax levied a fine of £14,000 on the town for harbouring the enemy. The town was in ruins from the bombardment and most people had lost everything, so they begged for help – so Fairfax reduced the fine to £12,000 (which was still equivalent to more than £1.2 million of today's money).

Lucas and Lisle were executed behind the castle at 7 p.m. on 28 August 1648. Lucas' last words were, 'See, I am ready for you; and now,

Monument to Charles Lucas and George Lisle in the castle grounds, Colchester.

rebels, do your worst.' Lisle followed him with, 'Shoot rebels; your shot, your shame; our fall, our fame.'

It's said that grass won't grow on the area where they were shot (not surprisingly, nowadays, as it's paved over! – though the story was also told by the diarist John Evelyn in July 1656) and a small obelisk marks the spot, put up in 1883.

Humpty Dumpty

It's said that the origins of the 'Humpty Dumpty' nursery rhyme lie in Colchester. During the siege in the Civil War, there was a Royalist gunner called One-Eyed Jack Thompson. Because of his shape, he was known as Humpty Dumpty, and he sat in the belfry of the church of St Mary-at-the-Walls (i.e. 'Humpty Dumpty sat on the wall'). He was shot down (Humpty's 'great fall') and the Parliamentarians won the town shortly afterwards. An alternative version says that 'Humpty Dumpty' was the name of the cannon placed at the top of the church on 15 June 1648, which was blown up on 15 July.

Scandal: James Parnell, the Quaker Martyr

In 1656 the young Quaker James Parnell was martyred at Colchester Castle. He was born at Retford in Nottinghamshire in 1636; he met George Fox, the founder of Quakers, in jail in Carlisle, then travelled south and started to spread the word. In 1655, he arrived at Colchester and began preaching. He was arrested at Coggeshall and charged with blasphemy, then taken to Colchester castle and imprisoned. At his trial in Chelmsford, he was acquitted and fined £40, but he refused to pay the fine and was returned to Colchester. The jailer, Nicholas Roberts, was cruel and corrupt, and the living conditions at the castle were atrocious. It's said that he was forced to climb a rope to get his food. Parnell became ill, and by spring 1656 he was too weak to eat. He died on 4 May 1656 and was buried in an unmarked grave. A memorial plaque commemorates him at his former cell in the castle.

Destruction and Rescue

Local businessman John Wheely bought the castle in 1683 and planned to demolish it and use it as building material ; however, after he'd removed part of the top storeys, he went bankrupt and the demolition ceased. In 1727, Charles Gray (later Colchester's MP) was given the castle as a wedding present. He restored it but, thinking that it was a Roman castle, added an Italianate façade and tower as well as a red

Vault where Parnell died in Colchester Castle.

roof. He also made a park round the castle and built a summer house in the shape of a Roman temple on the old Norman earthworks.

The castle and grounds were given to the town in 1892; the Upper and Lower Castle Parks remain as recreation grounds, and the castle became a museum in 1860, firstly with the crypt opening and eventually the entire building. It was restored by the local council in the 1930s and again between 1983-1992.

Spooks

James Parnell allegedly haunts the castle; so the story goes, a man full of bravado once stayed the night in the dungeons, saying he wasn't bothered about seeing the ghosts, but he came out the next morning a gibbering wreck.

Siege: Boudica's rebellion

The first permanent legionary fortress built by the Romans was at Colchester. However, when Boudica and her rebels sacked Colchester in AD 60, the Roman historian Tacitus claims that the city was undefended and there were only 200 soldiers garrisoned there.

Boudica was the queen of the Iceni, a tribe of East Anglia. Her husband, Prasutagus, was one of the client kings – because he didn't resist the Roman occupation in AD 43, he was allowed to keep his lands and continued to rule his people. This saved the Roman empire the expense of garrisoning the area and the client king kept the peace. When he died in AD 60, he left half his estates to his wife and daughters and the other half to Nero – clearly recognising that there needed to be a transition period while his kingdom was integrated into Roman Britain.

However, the Romans weren't happy about this; they wanted everything. They seized the throne, sacked Thetford, publicly whipped Boudica and raped her daughters. According to Tacitus, all the chief men of the Iceni were also stripped of their estates and the king's relatives were treated as slaves. There was already resentment at Roman rule (particularly by those chosen to be priests at the temple, who quickly discovered that it meant giving all their wealth to the temple's service), and the treatment meted out to the Iceni inflamed the situation.

The Roman governor, Suetonius Paulinus, was busy leading a campaign in Anglesey, North Wales; Boudica chose that moment to lead the rebellion, joining forces with the Trinovantes of Essex. According to the historian Dio Cassius, writing in the third century, Boudica was an imposing figure: 'huge of frame, terrifying of aspect, and with a harsh voice', with knee-length bright red hair. She spoke to her people about the Roman rule and how it would have been better to be sold into slavery than to have most of their lands taken and having to pay huge taxes on the rest.

Her first target was Colchester – the Colonia Victricensis of the Romans – where the veteran legionaries had driven the natives from their homes and called them captives and slaves. In the town, there were plenty of omens – the statue of Victory apparently fell unexpectedly, as if in retreat from the enemy, and a vision of the

Statue of Boudica at Westminster Bridge. Photograph by author.

ruined army barracks had been seen in the Thames. Others said that the sea looked blood-red and when the tide ebbed it left what looked like human corpses behind. The Romans saw the omens as danger, and Boudica's 100,000-strong army saw them as victory.

Although the Romans living in the city had enough time to send a message to Catus Decianus, the procurator (financial official), asking for help, they didn't evacuate the city. Catus sent 200 soldiers to help the small garrison in the town, but they didn't secure the ramparts. Boudica's army prevailed, and although the soldiers barricaded themselves into the temple, they were only able to hold it for two days. The rebels burned Colchester to the ground, and any digging in Colchester reveals a layer of red soot known as 'Boudica's Destruction Horizon', which is up to 30cm deep in places. Clay walls and foundations were baked solid, and the remains include grain, flax, coriander, lentils and even a bag of 22 dates and a plum (the only ones known from Roman Britain) have been found in the layer.

Petilius Cerealis arrived with the Ninth Legion, but Boudica's army routed them – and Catus fled to Gaul.

Next was London (Londinium). Suetonius Paulinus marched back from Anglesey, but decided that London could be sacrificed for the sake of the whole country – and the same went for St Albans (Verulamium). Boudica's rebels burned the city and slaughtered the inhabitants; Tacitus says in his *Annals* that around 70,000 Romans and their allies were killed in Colchester, London and St Albans. Some historians have suggested that the Walbrook Skulls may have belonged to Londoners killed by Boudica's army; however, as they belonged to young and middle-aged adults (not women and the elderly, whom Tacitus said were killed at London) and have no jaw bones, it's more likely that they were put in the river after the rebellion, probably as part of a ritual.

After St Albans, the rebels came face to face with Roman army at Watling Street, north of Verulamium. Boudica's army was 230,000 strong by this point, outnumbering the Romans by more than 20 to 1; however, the Romans had better discipline and better firepower, with barbed javelins and scorpios (which hurled bolts). They used a wedge formation to crush the rebels; Tacitus said that the Romans lost 400 men and the Britons lost 80,000 in the bloodbath.

And what happened to Boudica? Dio Cassius says that she fell ill and died; Tacitus says that she poisoned herself.

It's not known for certain where her grave is. After Lewis Spence published *Boadicea, Warrior Queen of the Britons* in 1937 saying that the battle was in the valley between St Pancras and King's Cross stations, people started to assume that her grave was under platform 9 at King's Cross – even though Spence didn't say she was buried on the site, and there is no archaeological evidence to show that she was buried there.

❊ ❊ ❊

Colchester Crossed Friars

The Friary of Colchester Crossed (or Crutched) Friars (OS map reference TL9911 2495) is the remains of the friary belonging to the Crossed Friars. It was founded by William de Lanvelli in the mid-thirteenth century as a friary and the hospital of the Holy Cross.

By 1401 the nave, chancel and bell tower of church all needed repair; the order was very poor and relied on begging and charitable donations for support. Around this time, the friars were pushed out; the hospital became a secular one and in 1407 the Guild of St Helen was founded in the church.

In 1496, the Crutched Friars (under the leadership of Roger Churche) protested that they'd been forced out; they showed charters and Papal bulls as evidence of their rights to the building. The Earl of Oxford got them reinstated and Roger became the prior.

The friary was dissolved in 1538 and the lands were granted to Thomas Audeley. The chapel was demolished and the house became the residence of the Stephens family and then Sir Harbottle Grimston, the MP for Colchester. It was severely damaged during the Siege of 1648; in 1700 the site was leased by the Workhouse Commission and the buildings (plus a large amount of new construction) became a workhouse. Later, it was let out as tenements, but then it was decided that the rents were not worth collecting and the building was pulled down.

The foundations of the friary were discovered in 1928 when 44 Crouch Street was demolished to build a new garage.

Scandal: the Murderer who took Sanctuary

In 1526 the friary was the centre of a row over sanctuary. William Gilbank, a murderer, originally took sanctuary in St John's Abbey; but then the broke sanctuary and went to the Crossed Friars instead. Sir John Vere went to the friary and asked the prior to give him up so Wolsey could examine him, but the prior refused and said that the friary had the same rights of sanctuary as St John's and it could not be broken. Vere again went to the friars; Gilbank finally confessed felony to the coroner, but Vere advised the coroner to defer abjuration (time for the accused to plead for pardon) until he'd spoken with Wolsey.

Excavations

Excavations in 1988 on the site of Birkitt Long solicitors revealed part of a medieval building, and further excavations around 2007 showed that the church of the friars was on Crouch Street where a new block of flats was built.

Colchester Priory (St Botolph)

Colchester Priory (OS map reference TL 9995 2497) is the remains of the first Augustinian priory built in England. The remains are part of the west front (which contains a lot of Roman brickwork) and the nave; it was built from flint and reused Roman bricks, then plastered and probably painted.

The priory is under the care of English Heritage and is open to the public.

The Beginning of the Priory

The priory may be built on the site of a former Roman cemetery church, and was at one point an Anglo-Saxon minster. The priory of St Julian and St Botolph was established at some time between 1093 and 1100 and a Kentishman called Norman, who had been studying in France, came to join the community. Shortly afterwards, the priests decided to join a religious order and asked Norman's advice as to which one they should choose. He suggested the Augustinians, and said that two of the priests should be sent to France to learn the rules.

Anselm, the archbishop of Canterbury, gave Norman a letter to recommend him to the abbot of Mont St Elois, so Norman took a companion with him to France. He studied at Chartres and Beauvais, then returned to teach at Colchester; this was probably before 1100 as the first grant to the priory was by William Rufus. Norman left in 1108 to become the first prior of Holy Trinity in Aldgate, London.

There is a papal bull of 1116 which recognises St Botolph's as the first Augustinian house in England, and said that it should have authority over all other Augustinian houses in England.

Scandal: Riots with St John's

There was a huge rivalry between St Botolph's and St John's and several disputes about territory. In the middle of the fourteenth

Colchester Priory.

century, the abbot of St John's complained to the Pope that John, the prior of St Botolphs, together with John Noreys and Thomas de Gipwico (two of his canons) and several laymen, attacked one of their monks with swords and daggers and blockaded them in the abbey. They also claimed that John had instigated a third canon and some laymen to enter the abbey and injure the abbot and monks. The pope said that if this was true, they'd be excommunicated. Nothing

Colchester Priory; plate from Thomas Kitson Cromwell's Excursions Through Essex, *1818-9.*

further is noted, so either the abbey and the priory sorted the matter out between them (as they did with some disputes the following year), or it was an exaggeration on the part of the abbot.

Scandal: forgery

In 1380, the prior and canons complained to the king that several people had collected money in their name through forged letters. The king ordered the arrest of the forgers and said that the letters should be delivered to the archbishop of Canterbury and the forgers should be sent to Newgate gaol.

The End of the Priory

The priory was dissolved in 1536 and many of the buildings were demolished. The church remained in the hands of the parish and the rest was granted to Sir Thomas Audeley. The Norman church was ruined during the Siege of Colchester in 1648, and in the eighteenth and nineteenth centuries the nave was used for burials.

✣ ✣ ✣

Cressing Preceptory

Cressing Preceptory (OS map reference TL799 186) is the site of the earliest English Knights Templar settlement. The only remains now are a stone well and two barns, which are thought to be the two finest Templar barns in Europe. The Barley Barn (dating from 1206) is the oldest timber-framed barn in the world. The Preceptory is owned by Essex County Council and is open to the public.

The barley barn at Cressing.
Photograph by author.

The Beginnings of the Preceptory

The land is thought to have belonged to King Harold before the Norman Conquest. It passed to Eustace of Bologne and from him to his daughter Matilda (Stephen's queen), who donated it to the Knights Templar in 1137. It's therefore thought that Cressing is one of the original Templar properties in England, along with Old Temple in London and Temple Cowley in Oxfordshire.

The wheat barn at Cressing. Photograph by author.

The Preceptory was united with Witham some time before 1250, but in 1312 the Order of the Templars was suppressed by Pope Clement V. He accused the Templars of blasphemy, heresy and witchcraft, though the accusations were never substantiated; more importantly, Philip IV of France (who persuaded Clement to suppress the order) was deeply in debt to them, so the suppression of the order was a financial necessity for him.

The Pope ordered that the Templar properties should be transferred to the Knights Hospitallers (aka the Order of the Knights of the Hospital of St John at Jerusalem, who were founded to provide medical care for pilgrims to the Holy Land).

The Uprising of 1381

The Preceptory was under the charge of a warden in 1381 when it was plundered during the Uprising. Sir Robert Hales was the Master of the Knights Hospitaller and was also Treasurer of England; he was universally loathed as the man who came up with the idea of the Poll Tax. Cressing was described in a contemporary document, the *Anonimalle Chronicle* as a 'fine and pleasant manor' which was 'well supplied with wines and suitably stocked'.

On 10 July 1381 a mob came to hang Hales, but discovered that he was in London. In response, they stole food and wine (apparently they drank three casks of wine), then demolished buildings and burned them. They also burned documents and carried off armour, money and vestments. Four days later, the rebels dragged Hales from the Tower of London and executed him.

The End of the Preceptory

The Preceptory became a private farm in 1515 when the Order leased it to John Edmondes. It was suppressed in 1540 and the site passed to Sir John Smyth (Baron of the Exchequer), whose family remodelled the buildings.

It then passed through several changes of owner. In 1913, the seed merchant Frank Cullen bought it; he maintained the buildings and modernised the farm with electricity and piped water.

Since then the Preceptory has starred in TV programmes including *Lovejoy*, *Top Gear* and the *Antiques Roadshow*.

Excavations

The site was excavated by J. H. Hope between 1978 and 1981. He discovered the chapel, a possible hall, several burials and an oven which contained twelfth-century shell-tempered pottery, oyster shell and animal bone (mainly pig bone).

Tunnels

There is a bricked-up doorway in the wall of the well, which is said to have been a priesthole for hiding catholic priests. Another suggestion says that it's an escape tunnel to Hungry Hall, a building half a mile away. However, as it contains Victorian bricks, it's most likely to be to do with drainage in the late 1800s.

The well at Cressing. Photograph by author.

Spooks

It's said that in 1949-50 people could hear the church organ being played at Cressing in the winter months, even though the church was locked and dark at the time. Two firemen from Braintree watched the church for two nights and heard nothing.

Children have seen the Hall Man at the Preceptory, at the top of the stairs; he has long dark hair, blue trousers and large boots.

One of the barns is allegedly haunted by an ostler who was killed by his horse. The horse used to walk around on top of the wheat or barley stacks to compress them, so more stacks could be put in; he had to be lifted out by block and tackle, and kicked the ostler in the head while he was in the hoist.

There's a very sad story of another horse that performed the same function in the mid-1800s. He disappeared and the farmhands thought that he'd been stolen; however, three months later they heard a horse whinnying and discovered that their horse had slipped down between the barley and the back wall. They cut a hole in the wall to get him out, but the horse was terrifically thirsty – he bolted over to the pond and drank his fill. However, he'd eaten plenty of corn during his time stuck in the barn, and the water caused the corn to swell inside him and he died.

❊ ❊ ❊

Earls Colne Priory

Earls Colne Priory (OS map reference TL864 289) is the remains of a Benedictine monastery dedicated to St Mary and St Andrew (though it's also known as the priory of St Mary the Virgin and St John the Evangelist, as it was rededicated in 1148). The remains are the base of the north-west church tower and a single stone from the presbytery. There is a house nearby called The Priory but it isn't completely on the site. It's also possible that the priory was built on the site of a Roman villa.

St Andrew's church, Earls Colne.
Photograph by author.

Beginnings of the Priory

The priory was founded by Aubrey de Vere and his wife Beatrice in about 1107 after the death of their eldest son, Godfrey. Godfrey had been cured of an illness by Faritius, the abbot of Abingdon, but had died from a different illness and was buried at the abbey in Abingdon. He left the grant of a church to Abingdon, but because it was so far from Essex his parents decided to found a cell to the abbey of Abingdon at Earl's Colne instead. The king and the Bishop of London agreed, and the charter was confirmed in 1111. Originally, twelve monks lived there.

Eventually problems arose between Abingdon and Colne, because Abingdon kept recalling the learned monks from Colne and replacing them with ignorant ones from Abingdon and charged Colne for all the travel expenses! In 1311 the Earl of Oxford mediated between them and it was agreed that the prior didn't have to consult the abbot of Abingdon and could let whoever he pleased be a monk.

Scandals: the Kidnapped Prior

At the end of the fourteenth century there was a huge row when the monks elected Henry Colne (aka Henry Kebbel) as their prior. Maud, the Countess of Oxford and patron of the priory, objected to the appointment. The king told the Bishop of London to sort it out; Henry resigned, and the bishop told the monks to elect someone else. They refused, so the bishop confirmed Henry as the prior on 6 May 1395. But in the meantime the Archbishop of Canterbury had already made John Preston the prior. Henry appealed to Rome, but John won the case. However, Henry was resident in the priory and refused to give it up. He appealed to the bishop, who decided in his favour – but John's supporters refused to accept the decision.

Henry IV was forced to step in and ordered a commission. Prior Henry complained that the Countess, John Preston and others had broken into the priory at night and carried him off 'shamefully clad'; they kept him imprisoned until he swore on the Host that he would let John Preston be prior and wouldn't tell anyone that he'd been forced to swear the oath. But then the Countess counter-complained that Henry and John Sudbury had committed trespass – and Henry didn't turn up to defend himself. John Preston asked for six of the monks (Henry Kebbel, John Sudbury, John Serle, Martin de Colne, John Colne and John Okelee – half the monks in the house) to be arrested as apostate (i.e. claiming that they'd renounced their religious life) in April 1399, but clearly this was part of the power struggle over the priorship than real apostasy, as Kebbel and Sudbury were released within a week.

Scandal: the Apostate Monks

In 1368 Ralph de Pelham was arrested as an apostate; however, he was reconciled with the priory by the pope and returned to his religious life.

The End of the Priory

Prior Robert Abell took the oath of supremacy in 1384 and in 1536 the site was granted to John de Vere, Earl of Oxford. De Vere sold the manor and then the priory to his steward, Richard Harlackenden. Between 1592-1631 most of the buildings were demolished and tomb monuments were taken to the parish church. After the property was sold in the eighteenth century to John Wale, the rest of the priory was demolished and Wale cut a ha-ha through the ruins, destroying part of the graveyard. He also built a house in 1740 and used de Vere tombs as fireplace surrounds! This house was demolished in 1827 and some of the materials were reused in the present house. Part of the north-west tower of the priory remained until 1988.

Spooks: the Phantom Bell

There is a legend of a phantom bell at Colne Priory. The story was written down by Richard Baxter in 1691. He said that he'd had a letter from Thomas Woodcocke, a tutor, saying that his boss, Mr Harlackenden, lived at Colne Priory; the butler and coachman slept in the room over the tomb house, and were always woken at 2 a.m. by the sound of the bell. One night, Mr Harlackenden got a servant to wake him at 1 a.m. and lay between his two servants; sure enough, an hour later, he heard the sound of the bell tolling. He then spent a night in prayer with ministers to cast out the devil, and from then on there was no sound from the bell.

Great Canfield Castle

Great Canfield Castle (OS map reference TL595 179) is the remains of a castle; only the earthworks can be seen, to the south-east of the church. There is a moated mount (45 feet high and 275 feet across at the base) plus a horseshoe-shaped bailey to the south.

The Beginnings of the Castle

A timber motte and bailey castle was built at Great Canfield by the de Veres in the late eleventh century. It's thought that in the 1130s Aubrey de Vere II diverted a stream to flood the ditch around the motte and built a dam to help reinforce it. According to excavations, the ditch was 20 feet deep, but the moat is now dry.

'Robert's Castle' was recorded in 1052; Robert Fitz Wymarc held the land before the conquest, so this reference may be to Great Canfield, but is more likely to refer to Clavering (see page 37).

Aubrey de Vere III supported Empress Maud against Stephen and in 1142 joined the plot of Geoffrey de Mandeville against Stephen; however, when Stephen arrested him at St Albans, Aubrey had to surrender Canfield to Stephen to regain his freedom.

The End of the Castle

It's not known when the castle was dismantled. During the mid-nineteenth century, according to the historian Duffield Coller, the castle-yard was used as a two-acre orchard.

The site of Great Canfield Castle. Photograph by author.

Hadleigh Castle

Hadleigh Castle (OS map reference TQ8101 8605) is a thirteenth-century stone keep and bailey fortress overlooking the Thames estuary. It is in the care of English Heritage and is open to the public. Pevsner calls it 'the most important later medieval castle in the country'.

The Beginnings of the Castle

It was founded by Hubert de Burgh in the thirteenth century (possibly using stone from Rayleigh – see page 102). De Burgh was the Regent for Henry III and was the justiciar of England as well as the Earl of Kent.

A licence to crenellate was given in 1230; the idea was to stop French invaders getting to London, and also to stop raiders attacking ships in the Thames estuary. Although Hubert de Burgh helped to draw up the terms of the Magna Carta, he remained loyal to King John.

Hadleigh Castle; plate from Thomas Kitson Cromwell's Excursions Through Essex, *1818-9.*

Betrayal of Hubert de Burgh

Soon after work began on the castle, de Burgh's enemies made false claims to the king, especially about his wealth – there was a lot of jealousy there because he had estates in fifteen counties, was sheriff of seven counties and was constable of three castles. They also said that he'd given Henry bad advice. Henry was angry about the failure of the French campaign (which de Burgh, incidentally, had advised against) and blamed de Burgh.

De Burgh decided to go to live in Norfolk until things settled down. He stopped at Brentwood, but was recognised by his enemies, who tried to arrest him. He went to Becket's chapel and claimed sanctuary (meaning that he could stay there for 40 days without being harmed, could have food and water brought to him, and if he surrendered he could either stand trial or leave the country), but the soldiers sent to arrest him broke sanctuary and dragged him out. The blacksmith who was meant to put iron shackles on him refused to do so, so the soldiers tied him up themselves, put him on a horse and took him to London. However, the Bishop of London was angry that the terms of sanctuary had been broken and let de Burgh go back to Brentwood to sanctuary.

Hadleigh Castle. Photograph by author.

Henry's soldiers kept a watch to ensure that de Burgh couldn't escape or tunnel out of the chapel; they also stopped food and drink going in to him, so eventually he was forced to surrender. They put him in the Tower of London, and Henry III seized all his castles. However, eight months later, Henry changed his mind and gave de Burgh his lands back. De Burgh died in 1243 and Hadleigh started to fall into disrepair, suffering from landslips.

Remodelling

In the mid-1360s Edward III decided to use the castle to help defend against the threat of French raids. He repaired and remodelled the castle, adding round towers to the curtain wall and building royal apartments. Documents relating to the building work of 1365-6 still exist, showing that he spent £2,287 (equivalent to nearly £850,000 in modern terms) on the castle. The stone and sand came from Kent; chalk and plaster came from London; wood and tiles came from Thundersley, Bicknacre and Little Baddow; boards came from East Hanningfield and Maldon; straw came from Benfleet; and glass came from Rayleigh. The mortar also contains cockleshells from Canvey Island.

Hadleigh was the dower of several queens, including Edward IV's wife Elizabeth Woodville, and three of Henry VIII's wives – Catherine of Aragon, Anne of Cleves and Catherine Parr. Anne lived at Hadleigh after her divorce from Henry.

The End of the Castle

Edward VI sold the castle for £700 (equivalent to £150,000 in modern terms) to Lord Rich of Leez Priory in 1551. Rich used the stone, and the castle was in ruins by the seventeenth century. Most of the south side has slipped.

Constable visited Hadleigh in 1814 and made sketches of the scenery. He wrote to his fiancée Maria Bicknell about the discovery: 'I have found perfection. At

Hadleigh there is the ruin of a castle, which, from its situation, is vastly fine. It commands a view of the Kent hills, the Nore, and the North Foreland, looking many miles to sea.' He finally painted the castle in 1829.

Spooks: Wryneck Sal

It's said that a milkmaid once met a ghost at the castle. The white lady asked her to return and promised to tell her mysteries about the place. The milkmaid was terrified and she didn't come back; the angry ghost found her, the next day, and slapped her for not doing what she was told – and the milkmaid was known as 'wryneck Sal' after then.

Spooks: Cunning Murrell, the last Witch Doctor in England

James Murrell – known as Murrell the Cunning Man – was born in Hadleigh in 1812, the seventh son of a seventh son. He was a herbalist who only travelled by night; he gathered plants by moonlight and hung them from his umbrella. It was said that he had a mirror that could show where property had been lost and a magic telescope that could see through walls, plus a copper bracelet on his wrist to detect dishonest men. He called himself the Devil's Master and claimed that he could exorcise spirits and lift curses.

One of his habits was to make witch bottles to cure people. One poor girl starting barking like a dog and her family thought that she'd been was cursed by a gipsy woman. Murrell made one of his witch bottles and heated it; it exploded, and the next morning the girl was back to normal and the gipsy was found face down in her fire.

Murrell allegedly foretold his death – on 16 December 1860 – and he was buried in Hadleigh church in an unmarked grave. Another version of the story says that Murrell was born in Rochford in 1780 and was a shoemaker and cunning man in Hadleigh by 1810. Some people thought he was a smuggler, whereas others believed that he was a good man who helped others. His death certificate describes him as a 'quack doctor' who died from natural causes.

According to Simpson and Westwood, when Murrell was detecting thieves, he made suspects go through a dark room and touch a pot smeared with oil and blacking. He told them that the cockerel under the pot would crow when it was touched by guilty person; when the cock didn't crow, Murrell examined their hands and the guilty person usually had clean hands!

Smugglers

There are legends that the castle was haunted; people used to see lights flashing but they were actually signals from smugglers. There were allegedly tunnels between the castle and the river, used by the smugglers, but there is no trace of them now.

Hatfield Broadoak Priory

Hatfield Broadoak Priory (OS map reference TL5470 1662) is the remains of an Augustinian monastery dedicated to St Mary. The remains include the parish church of St Mary, which was the nave of the original priory church, plus remains of the former presbytery and central tower.

Beginnings of the Priory

Before 1066, there was a wooden Saxon church on the site, measuring around 80 feet by 40 feet. The priory was founded by Aubrey de Vere II around 1135 as

Hatfield Broad Oak church; plate from Thomas Kitson Cromwell's Excursions Through Essex, *1818-9.*

a cell to the abbey of St Melaine at Rennes in Brittany; he extended the original church eastwards by building a Norman tower, the monks' choir and various chapels, plus cloisters and domestic offices to the north of the church. His son confirmed the grant, and the deed is sealed with a small broken knife attached to a harp string.

St Mary the Virgin's church, Hatfield Broad Oak. Photograph by author.

Effigy of Robert de Vere, Third Earl of Oxford, St Mary the Virgin's church, Hatfield Broad Oak. Robert was a great benefactor to the monastery and died in 1221, although the effigy was not placed in front of the high altar of the monastery until around 1270. After Dissolution, it's thought that the effigy was moved to the parish church, though it spent some time outside (which removed the colour from the effigy) and it was only moved to its present position in 1891. Photograph by author.

Fire

In 1230, part of the priory church was destroyed by fire. Henry III had been at Hatfield the previous year, and granted the prior some oaks from the Forest of Hatfield plus more from Writtle to help repair the church.

Scandal: Fight for Independence

There were many fights between the priory and St Botolph's in Colchester over tithes; every so often, they ended up in court and peace reigned for a little while after the judgement.

A huge row broke out in 1235 when the abbot of St Melaine said that he had the right to appoint the prior, but the Earl of Oxford, who was the priory's patron, said that he was the one with the right of appointment.

The monks sided with the abbot, so when the earl appointed William, a monk of Colchester, as the prior, the monks objected; the bishop promptly excommunicated them and anyone who took communion with them. The abbot asked the bishop to relieve the sentence; he refused, and the earl put the priory under armed guard. The abbot then appealed to the pope.

Meanwhile, William removed the priory's treasure and its books. When an archdeacon asked him to give the monks what was necessary, he agreed, but told his ministers to serve them like swineherds instead of monks, told the cooks not to give them fire or water, made the lay brothers and servers swear not to give the monks anything, and closed the dormitory so the monks were forced to go back to Rennes.

Eventually, they came to a settlement in 1254, and the priory became independent of Rennes.

Remaining piers from the priory at the east end of the church, Hatfield Broad Oak. Photograph by author.

Siege: Attack on the Priory

Thanks to the generosity of Robert Taper and his wife Millicent, the priory was extended in the fourteenth century. When the parishioners decided to restore the parish church, a row broke out between them and the monks. Things got so bad that in 1378 the prior complained that the vicar of Hatfield and a mob had attacked the priory, knocked down much of the cloister and the walls, and thrown the monks out. They appealed to the king, but clearly Richard II sympathised with the parish in this case because he ordered that they should build a wall across the nave to separate the parish and priory churches. This wall is the present east wall of the church (see picture above).

The End of the Priory

Prior Richard took the Oath of Supremacy in July 1534. The priory was dissolved in 1536 and the site was granted to Thomas Noke of Hatfield. The domestic priory buildings, which were on the north side of the church, were pulled down, and the stone was reused. In 1897 the area was excavated but covered up again to preserve the remains.

✢ ✢ ✢

Hatfield Peverel Priory

Hatfield Peverel Priory (OS map reference TL707 109) was a Benedictine monastery dedicated to St Mary. The only remains are the nave of the church, which became the parish church.

The Beginnings of the Priory

Originally the priory was a college of secular canons, founded by Ingelrica, the wife of Ranulph Peverel, around 1086. So the story goes, she was a celebrated beauty of her time, and William the Conqueror fell in love with her and made her his mistress; she had a son by him, and allegedly she founded the college to atone for her sins, dedicating it to St Mary Magdalene. She apparently lived there until her death near the end of the century; according to Daniel Defoe, she was buried in the parish church and a tombstone to her memory was set up under a window.

After her death, her son William converted the college into a Benedictine monastery, as a cell to St Albans, and dedicated it to St Mary the Virgin.

Fire

Matthew Paris's chronicle records that on 16 March 1231 there was a serious fire that destroyed much of the priory; only the chapel, barns and granary were saved. Apparently all the metal objects in the priory, including the bells, were melted.

Church of St Andrew, Hatfield Peverel. Photograph by author.

Scandal

In 1230, during the abbot's visitation, the monks complained hugely about Alexander de Burgo, the prior; the abbot decided that the monks were justified and removed him from office.

There were obviously local troubles, as William de Huntendune of St Albans was sent to Rome to ask the pope to stop other bishops claiming visitation rights.

There were other disputes over tithes – notably with Sir Andrew de Nevile over the church of Assington in 1290 and with Debden in 1341 (both of which the priory won) and with Beeleigh over Ulting in 1510 (where rights were split between the two sides).

The End of the Priory

The priory was dissolved in 1536 and most of the buildings were pulled down (although a map of 1765 shows 'the old priory' on the south of the east end of the church, and 'the kitchen' on the south east'). The nave was used as the parish church. The site was granted to Giles Leigh; a house known as 'the priory' was built nearby in 1775.

During drainage work in 1976, an Elizabethan well was discovered plus a human burial.

Spooks: the Ghostly Dog

There is a legend in Hatfield Peverel of a ghostly dog, which used to haunt a quiet lane. Although the dog resembled Old Shuck, it was harmless, happy just to walk up and down the lane. One local lad, driving back from market, decided that he'd try to liven things up and see if the dog was like the one that haunted Norfolk and Suffolk, and slashed his whip across the poor dog's rear. The dog turned round, staring at the boy – and then a lightning bolt came down and reduced the lad, his cart and his two horses to smoking ashes.

The dog continued to walk up and down the lane after that, unbothered by the villagers – until early in the twentieth century, when the first motor car was seen in the village. As the car drew level with the dog, the beast wailed and exploded into flames… and has never been seen since.

The Witches of Hatfield Peverel

In July 1566, there was a witch trial at Chelmsford concerning several women from Hatfield Peverel; a pamphlet was published in London shortly afterwards detailing their confessions.

The first was Elizabeth Francis, who claimed that she'd been a witch since the age of 12 after being taught by her grandmother, Eve. Eve apparently gave her granddaughter a white spotted cat which had to be kept in a basket, fed with bread and milk, and was called Satan. Elizabeth asked for riches, and the cat (in a strange, hollow voice) asked her what she wanted; she asked for sheep, and was duly given 28 beasts, but they vanished. She also wanted to marry Andrew Byles; Andrew, however, refused to marry her, so she got the cat to ruin his business and then kill him. She then married Mr Francis and had a daughter by him – but she wasn't happy and told the cat to kill her child and make her husband lame. After fifteen years of living with the cat, she persuaded her neighbour Mrs Waterhouse to swap a cake for the cat. (In the 1566 pamphlet, their relationship is that of neighbour, but in the 1572 trials, it turns out that Agnes Waterhouse was Elizabeth's sister.)

Agnes Waterhouse, aged 64, confessed that she'd received the cat. She got him to kill one of her pigs, and gave him a chicken for doing it; when she fell out with her neighbour Mr Kersey, she asked the cat to kill three of his pigs, again rewarding him with chicken. There followed a whole list of fallings-out with her neighbours – involving a cow being drowned, three geese killed, brewing and butter-making ruined, another neighbour killed, and also her husband. She couldn't afford to keep the cat in a basket filled with white wool, so she prayed to God for it to be turned into a toad, and was then able to keep it in a pot.

Agnes Waterhouse's daughter Joan (age 18) was also examined and confessed that she'd seen her mother with the toad, and when her mother was absent one day she asked Agnes Brown, a neighbour's daughter, for bread and cheese – and, when refused it, asked the toad to scare the girl.

Agnes Brown claimed that she was visited by 'a thynge like a black dogge with a face like an ape, a short taile, a cheine and sylver whystle (to her thinking) about his neck, and a peyre of hornes on his head, and brought in his mouth the key of the milkehouse doore'. It terrified her, demanding butter, then turning up with variously a bean pod, a key, a piece of bread and then finally a knife. Agnes Waterhouse was asked what prayers she said, and answered 'the Lordes Prayer, the Ave Maria' – but admitted that she said it in Latin. So it may be that she simply hadn't converted to Protestantism, and her neighbours – who didn't follow the Catholic rituals and superstitions – used her unconventional behaviour against her.

Elizabeth Frances was sentenced to a year's imprisonment and pillory; she was up before the magistrates again on charges of witchcraft in 1572, and given the same punishment, but finally in 1579, on her third trial, she was executed); Agnes Waterhouse was executed.

Latton Priory

L atton Priory (OS map reference TL465 065) is the remains of an Augustinian priory dedicated to St John the Baptist which was founded some time during the twelfth century. The four crossing arches plus some of the walls of the priory church have been used as a barn for more than 200 years. The ruins are on private land and are not accessible to the public.

Beginning of the Priory

At the end of the thirteenth century there was a prior and two canons at Latton. In 1443 the Augustinian Chapter fined Latton 3s 4d each for not sending representatives to the chapter, and three years later the Northampton Chapter was informed that Latton had a prior and no canons.

Latton Priory; plate from Thomas Kitson Cromwell's Excursions Through Essex, *1818-9.*

The End of the Priory

Clearly the situation of only having a prior at the priory continued for a long time. At the inquisition on 9 September 1534 it was reported that John Taillour, late prior, 'had some time since voluntarily departed from it, leaving all to the will of the patron, and it had thus become a profane place'. It was dissolved and the site was granted to Sir Henry Parker.

Tunnels

In September 1960, a tunnel was said to have been found leading from the ruins of Latton Priory which was 'six feet high, and with little alcoves every twenty-five yards where you could sit and rest'.

Spooks and Visions

The doors of the barn are alleged to open by themselves at midnight – perhaps as they had before services in the Middle Ages

In 1931 Clive Luget published a children's book, *The Vision of Latton Priory*, where he and some friends visit the ruins of Latton Priory and see a vision of the monks in the middle ages. In the book, the monks are guardians of 'The Sacred Stone', which works miracles.

Shortly afterwards, Luget became the rector at Middleton, near Sudbury, and in 1932 several people in the village saw a bright, glowing ball of light there. Luget was one of the witnesses, and claimed that he'd seen the Virgin Mary and the Crucifixion in the light. Two days later, the organist, Francis Thornber, saw another light, and his seven-year-old son had a vision of Middle Church as it had been several hundred years before, with three people looking through an opening in the chancel wall. Luget asked the boy to mark the position on the wall, then scraped away the plaster and discovered a leper squint there.

The following year, Luget spoke of more visions of the Virgin Mary and said that he saw angels on a daily basis. A huge row blew up, with Philip Rand of the Protestant Trust Society holding meetings to protest about the Anglo-Catholic practices of Father Luget. Throughout, Luget continued to talk to people about his visions (albeit not to the press).

Although Luget became almost blind, he refused to have surgery, convinced that a healing spring would appear at Middleton that would restore his sight, and he would then build a monastery around it. The spring never rose; he retired in 1951 and died a few months later in Sudbury.

❊ ❊ ❊

Little Dunmow Priory

Little Dunmow Priory (OS map reference TL6560 2123) is the remains of an Augustinian Priory dedicated to St Mary the Virgin. The parish church is the former Lady Chapel of the priory. There are no remains above ground of the other monastic buildings.

The manor of Little Dunmow was held by the freewoman Ailish during the time of Edward the Confessor, but the land was granted to Ralph Baynard at the Conquest. Ralph's grandson, William, was involved with a rebellion against Henry I; when it failed, William was stripped of his estates and Little Dunmow was given to Richard Fitzgilbert, who founded the Fitzwalter family. Both the Baynards and the Fitzwalters have strong connections with the church and the priory.

The Beginnings of the Priory

The priory was founded by Juga Baynard, Ralph Baynard's sister, who persuaded the Bishop of London to dedicate it to St Mary. Around 1106 her son, Geoffrey Baynard, put canons in the church and it became a priory of the Augustinians. It had about a dozen canons and, according to Morant, was fairly large. It took a century to build and additions were made during its lifetime. The church was used by the parish as well as the priory.

St Mary's church, Little Dunmow: the former lady chapel of Little Dunmow Priory.
Photograph by author.

Scandals

In 1268 Prior John was suspended for four days for not paying tithes, but was reinstated after an appeal. There was a further scandal in 1369 when an order was sent out on 29 August to arrest William de Stoke, a canon of Dunmow; apparently he had been counterfeiting money! A warrant for the arrest of Richard Mylyent was sent out in 1458; Richard was accused of becoming apostate, i.e. giving up the religious life without permission.

The Dunmow Flitch

The Dunmow Flitch is believed to have been instigated by Robert Fitzwalter. The idea was that any man who hadn't repented of his marriage (either sleeping or waking) for a year and a day could go to Dunmow and claim a flitch (gammon) of bacon.

The applicant had to take oath before the prior and convent and the whole town, humbly kneeling in the churchyard upon two hard pointed stones, and he was then paraded in the chair through the

Flitch Kneelers in St Mary's church, Little Dunmow. Photograph by author.

priory and the town. The ceremony is referenced in two seminal medieval texts. The first is Langland's *Piers Plowman* (Passus IX, lines 166-71), dating from 1377:

In jelousie joyelees and janglynge on bedde,
Many a peire sithen the pestilence han plight hem togideres.
The fruyt that thei brynge forth arne [manye] foule words;
Have thei no children but cheeste and chopp[les] hem bitwene.
Theough thei do hem to Dunmowe, but if the devel helpe
To folwen after the flicche, fecche thei it nevere;
But thei bothe be forswore, that bacon they tyne.

Translation:
In jealousy joyless and quarrelling on bed
Many a pair since the plague have joined themselves together.
The fruit that they bring forth are many foul words;
Have they no children but fighting and blows them between.
Though they take themselves to Dunmow, unless the devil help
To follow after the flitch, fetch they it never;
Unless they both be foresworn, that bacon they lose.)

It also appears in Chaucer's Prologue to the *Bath of Wife's Tale*, dating ten years later:

I sette hem so a-werke, by my fey
That many a nyght they songen 'weilawey!'
The bacon was nat fet for hem, I trowe,
That som men han in Essex at Dunmowe.

Translation (lines 221-4):
I ruled them so, by my faith
That many a night they sang 'Alas!'
The bacon was not fetched for them, I believe,
That some men have in Essex at Dunmow.

The awards appear to have been given to husbands only, and three successful claims are recorded before the Dissolution. The first is yeoman Richard Wryght of Badeburgh [Bawburgh], near Norwich; he claimed the bacon on 17 April 1445, and was sworn according to the form of the charter before John Canon, the prior, plus the rest of the priory and neighbours, and was presented with a flitch. The second was husbandman Stephen Samuel, of Little Ayston, who came to the priory on Lady Day (25 March) 1467 and demanded a gammon. He was sworn before Roger Bulcott, the prior, plus the rest of the priory and neighbours. The third was John Ley, a fuller from Coggeshall, who came to the priory on Sunday 8 September 1510 and was sworn before John Tyler, the prior, plus the rest of the priory and neighbours.

The Flitch Chair in St Mary's church, Little Dunmow; this was probably originally the prior's chair.
Photograph by author.

The custom lapsed after the Dissolution and was revived in 1701. John and Anne Reynolds of Hatfield Broad Oak and William and Jane Parsley of Great Easton were awarded the bacon, and this was the first instance recorded as being judged by a jury of five spinsters.

In 1751, weaver Thomas Shakesshaft from Wethersfield and his wife were awarded the flitch – but they rather cheekily cut it into slices and sold it to people in the crowd, making a huge profit! There is an engraving by David Ogborne of them being carried away from the church on the chair, suspended on poles, with huge numbers of people in the crowds.

A newspaper report from 1772 says that on 12 June John and Susan Gilder of Tarling, Essex, gave notice that they wanted to claim the flitch; lots of people followed them to the church, but the priory gates were nailed shut and the lord of the manor refused to admit them.

Again, the custom lapsed, but in 1854 novelist Harrison Ainsworth published *The Flitch of Bacon, or The Custom of Dunmow, a Tale of English Home*. He then revived the custom of the flitch, offering a side of bacon, and moved the ceremony to Great Dunmow. A replica chair and kneeling stones are now used.

Ainsworth wrote a form of the oath in rhyme:

> *You shall swear by Custom of Confession,*
> *That you ne'er made nuptial transgression;*
> *Nor since you were married man and wife,*
> *By household brawls, or contentious strife,*
> *Or otherwise, at bed or at board,*

Offended each other in deed or in word
Or since the parish clerk said Amen,
Wished yourselves unmarried again;
Or in a Twelvemonth and a Day,
Repented not in thought any way;
But continued true and in desire,
As when you join'd hands in holy quire.
If to these Conditions, without all fear,
Of your own accord you will freely swear:
A whole Gammon of Bacon you shall receive,
And bear it hence with love and good leave;
For this is our Custom at Dunmow well-known:-
Though the pleasure be ours, the Bacon's your own.

Since the end of the Second World War, the flitch trials have been held every leap year; couples who have been married for at least a year and a day and who want to claim the bacon come to the court to submit their claim. A judge hears what they have to say, the 'opposing council' (representing the donors of the flitch) contest it, and a jury of six maidens and six bachelors make the final decision. Those who succeed are carried to the market place in the flitch chair, and those who don't succeed have to walk behind an empty chair. At the last trials (12 July 2008), four couples were successful in claiming the flitch, including a couple from Nashville in the US.

The End of the Priory

The priory was dissolved in 1534, and the site was granted to Robert Radcliffe, Earl of Sussex. The buildings were demolished soon afterwards.

Nicholas de Bromfeld, canon of Dunmow, who was born in 1259, wrote a chronicle during his time at the priory. The only copy still in existence is a later transcript by the historian John Stow.

The priory was excavated between 1913 and 1914 by Sir Alfred Clapham and Sir Mortimer Wheeler; they uncovered part of the foundation of the east wall of the presbytery, three graves, and foundations of the tower piers.

Matilda Fitzwalter, King John and Robin Hood

One of the tombs in the church is of Matilda Fitzwalter. Her father, Robert Fitzwalter, clashed badly with King John and was accused of plotting to kill the king in 1212. He certainly rebelled against John in 1212 because he besieged Binham Priory in Norfolk, that year, and John was furious, yelling, 'Ho, by God's feet, either I or Fitzwalter must be King of England!' The rebellion was quashed; Fitzwalter was outlawed and fled to France. He made peace with John in 1213, but rebelled again in 1214, joining the barons at Bury St Edmunds, and was one of the barons who forced John to sign the Magna Carta at Runnymede in 1215.

Matthew Paris wrote in the late thirteenth century that Robert Fitzwalter died on 8 December 1235 and was buried by the High Altar in Little Dunmow church. Paris also said that Fitzwalter had several children, including Matilda the Fair, who was said to be the real 'Maid Marion' and had been poisoned by King John.

Although 'Maid Marion' isn't part of the early Robin Hood legends, Anthony Munday rewrote the stories

Matilda Fitzwalter, aka Maid Marian – tomb in St Mary's church, Little Dunmow. Photograph by author.

as a play published in 1601 (*Death of Robert, Earle of Huntingdon, otherwise called Robin Hood of merrie Sherwood; with the lamentable tragedy of chaste Matilda, his faire maide Marion, poysoned at Dunmowe by King John*) and in this play Matilda Fitzwalter takes the alias of Marion. Robert Fitzwalter was married to Maud, daughter of the Earl of Huntingdon, so that's a possible explanation for the confusion.

Robert himself claimed that one of the reasons he rebelled against John was because John had tried to seduce his daughter. There's a local legend that, on Matilda's eighteenth birthday, her father held a three-day tournament at one of his castles. The victor vanished into Sherwood forest; when Matilda refused John's attentions, she escaped into the forest and was rescued by the man who won the tournament.

The two stories have become muddled over the years; allegedly, Matilda's husband was outlawed by King John and she was outlawed with him. When her husband died, she took refuge at the priory at Little Dunmow. However, John hadn't forgotten her, and he sent his knight Robert de Medewe to her with a bracelet. Unbeknown to de Medewe, the bracelet was poisoned. De Medewe was received kindly at Dunmow and fell in love with Matilda; on his way back to London, he changed his mind about going to the capital and decided to return to Dunmow. He arrived later that night, but saw that the church was lit with tapers and he could hear a funeral dirge being sung. When he went into the church, he saw Matilda's lifeless body there on a bier in the chancel; the poisoned bracelet had eaten its way through to her bone. De Medewe flung himself on her corpse, cursing himself – and, in penance for his actions, he became an Augustinian monk.

Another version of the story, in John Weever's *Ancient Funerall Monuments* (1631), says that after Matilda refused the king, she was locked in the Tower of London and was then given a poisoned boiled egg. However, the eighteenth-century Essex historian Philip Morant says 'the story appears to me a fiction', and the *Gentleman's Magazine* (1860) says that it was likely that Matilda was part of the Fitzwalter family, but not born before the time of Henry IV, nearly 200 years later.

Little Horkesley Priory

Little Horkesley Priory (OS map reference TL960 319) was a cell of the Cluniac monastery at Thetford in Norfolk and was dedicated to St Peter.

The Beginnings of the Priory

The priory was founded by Robert, son of Godebold, and his wife Beatrice in 1127. There are no real remains of the priory, though the architectural historian Nikolaus Pevsner believes that one wall of the house called 'The Priory', built next door to the church, was part of the original priory. The church of St Peter and St Paul, sited next door to the priory, was badly damaged by a German parachute mine in 1940; however, amazingly, three rare thirteenth-century wooden effigies survived and are still displayed in the church, which was rebuilt in 1958.

Scandals: the Vagabond Prior

During the visitation of 1279, it was reported that four monks and a prior lived there and 'led good lives' – though it's notable that in 1295, Prior Henry was acquitted of the charge of taking dogs and a bow and arrow to hunt a hare at Great Horkesley.

In the 1370s, there was a row between the monks at Horkesley and the monks at Thetford. John, the prior of Thetford, denounced Roger de Ware as a vagabond, and Edward III ordered Roger to be arrested and delivered to him. Roger protested that he'd been the prior at Horkesley for a long time, and added that the priory was no longer under the jurisdiction of Thetford. He appealed to Canterbury and Rome, and in October 1374 the king ordered the prior of Thetford to appear in the Chancery court. Roger clearly won the case because he was listed as the prior of Horkesley in 1388.

The End of the Priory

As one of the smaller monasteries, Horkesley was dissolved by Wolsey in 1525 and the funds used to support his college, firstly at Oxford and then in 1528 at Ipswich.

Wooden effigies from the church of St Peter and St Paul, Little Horkesley.
Photograph by author.

Little Leighs (or Leez) Priory

Leez Priory is a sixteenth-century house on the site of Little Leigh's priory (OS map reference TL7011 1855), which was an Augustinian priory dedicated to St Mary and St John the Evangelist. It is on private land and is used as a wedding venue.

The Beginnings of the Priory

The priory was founded by Ralph Gernon in the late twelfth century.

Scandals: Visitation

In 1309, clearly the priory was having problems with discipline, as the injunctions of Bishop Baldock survive. He said that the

Leez Priory; plate from Thomas Kitson Cromwell's Excursions Through Essex, 1818-9.

monks needed to attend all offices, give up their belongings and were not allowed to sell property, and had keep the rule of silence; if they broke it, they would be sentenced to bread and water for two days. He also said that no women were

Leez Priory. Photograph by author.

allowed in the priory, and the monks were not allowed to go into the wood or the town without the prior's consent; if he gave consent, they had to go 'with an honest companion'. They also weren't allowed to give their food to others outside the refectory, and had to keep the priory seal under a lock with three keys.

In 1342, the Prior of Leighs was prosecuted 'for enclosing a park called Proureswode, in Leighs, adjoining to the forest of Felstede, and hunting in the forest without warrant or authority'.

There was another row in 1405, when a local man and his wife claimed that they had a contract for a corrody with the priory that wasn't honoured – this was an early kind of insurance policy, where people could pay a sum of money to a religious house which would promise to give them a home, food and fuel when they were older.

In 1471, there was a row with the local JP, Sir Robert Wynkefeld, who took one of the priory's manors under a forged grant. When the prior sent canon Robert Colne there, Wynkefeld allegedly seized him and took goods and cattle belonging to the priory.

The End of the Priory

The priory was dissolved in 1536 and the canons were sent to Waltham Abbey. Lord Richard Rich was granted the site; he demolished the priory buildings and used the materials to build a house, which was itself partly demolished in 1753.

Local people weren't that happy with Dissolution. James Mallett, who'd been the rector of nearby Great Leighs for twenty-eight years and had once been chaplain to the queen, spoke out openly against the king's actions: 'Then hath the king brought his hogs to a fair market.' On market day, Friday 1 December 1542, Mallett was drawn, hanged and quartered for high treason.

Maldon Whitefriars

Maldon Whitefriars (OS map reference TL850 069) was a Carmelite friary. There are no remains above ground although there are some carved and moulded stones (dating from the thirteenth to the fifteenth centuries) built into a seventeenth-century wall in the garden of 'The Friary', but these may be from other buildings in the area. Priory Garden is in the care of the Maldon and Heybridge Horticultural Society, which has restored it, and there are open days once a month.

Maldon at low tide. Photograph by author.

The Beginnings of the Friary

The Carmeline friary was founded by Richard Gravesend, the Bishop of London, and Richard Isleham, the rector of South Hanningfield, in 1292.

Clashes with Beeleigh

In the early days of the friary, there were a fair amount of clashes with the abbot of Beeleigh, because the friary was situated in the parish of All Saints and the abbot was the rector of the church of All Saints. Eventually, in 1300, the bishop decreed that the friars should have a belfry and oratory where they could say Mass, and all tithes and offerings would continue to go to the church (and, more importantly, the abbot!). The friars were not allowed to bury anyone in their cemetery unless the family had requested it (without being influenced by the friars) and all dues had been paid to the church; they were also not allowed to hear confessions unless the curate had licensed them to do so, and not allowed to act as executors of wills. The friars had to pay the abbot 5 shillings of silver every year, and if they extended the friary they'd have to pay more to the abbot.

Scandals

In 1381, it was ordered that the friar Edmund Barnton (or Bramton) should be arrested and delivered to prior Thomas to be punished. He was accused of apostasy – in other words, of abandoning the religious life without permission from the head of his order.

The End of the Friary

Maldon Whitefriars was one of the poorest houses in England and was dissolved in 1538. The land was leased to William Harrys and then sold to George Duke and John Sterre in 1544, including 'le litle courtyard' and 'le priours garden'. A house was built on the site in 1570; it was demolished and the present house, The Friary, was built on the site around 1805-7. Excavations in 1990-1 showed the location of the cloister.

The Battle of Maldon

The site of the Battle of Maldon (OS Map Reference TL 871 058) is a registered battlefield and is the oldest battlefield recorded by English Heritage. The route to the site along the sea wall is part of the 22-mile walk called the Maldon Millennium Way, set up as part of the 1000th anniversary of the Battle of Maldon.

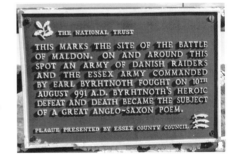

The plaque on the gate on the landward side of the sea wall, commemorating the Battle of Maldon. Photograph by author.

So what actually happened at the battle?

Sweyn Forkbeard led the main Viking raids to England in 991, with 4,000 men in 93 ships. They pillaged Folkestone, Sandwich, and Ipswich; but at Maldon they were met by Ealdorman Byrhtnoth and his forces. The Vikings camped on Northey Island, which is connected to the mainland by a narrow causeway which is usable at low tide and is covered over within two hours either side of high tide. Byrhtnoth and his forces protected the causeway, but then allowed the Vikings to come over and fight on the mainland – and lost.

The battle is commemorated in the Anglo-Saxon poem 'The Battle of Maldon', which is thought to have been composed around 1031. It's not known who commissioned it; however, Byrhtnoth's widow Aelflaed gave a tapestry to the monastery at Ely commemorating the battle, and it's tempting to think that she also commissioned the poem.

The marshes around the battlefield site.
Photograph by author.

The poem itself is a fragment of 325 lines. The original was destroyed in 1731 during by a fire in the Cotton library at Ashburnham House, where the manuscript was kept, but luckily John Elphinston had already made a transcript of the poem earlier in the eighteenth century. Given that the poem is fairly terse, there are probably only about 50 lines missing in total. It's very much stylised battle account and is thought to have been written very early in the tenth century, as it uses the original form of Byrhtnoth's name (he's often shown as 'Brithnoth').

At the beginning, Byrhtnoth orders his men to stand and shown them how to hold weapons. He orders them to 'send steed away and stride forwards' (ie they arrived on horseback and fought on foot. The leader of the Vikings promises to sail away if they buy him off with gold. But Byrhtnoth says:

Gehyrst þu, sælida,   hwæt þis folc segeð?
Hi willað eow to gafole   garas syllan,
Ættryne ord   and ealde swurd,
Þa heregeatu   þe eow æt hilde ne deah.

(Translation:Do you hear, seafarer, what these people say?
They will give you spears for tribute,
Poisonous points and tried sword-edge,
Your war-tax will not help you in the fight.)

The causeway between the mainland and Northey Island. Photograph by author.

84

Then the tide rises and the troops from both sides line the banks of the river Panta (nowadays known as the Blackwater). As soon as the tide ebbs again, Byrhtnoth asks Wulfstan, Maccus and Alfere to guard the causeway – which they do, and they do it so well that not a single Viking can cross the causeway. The Vikings then ask Byrhtnoth to let them come safely on to shore so they can fight there; he agrees, and tells his men to make a shield wall. Ravens and eagles circle overhead during the battle; men on both sides are lost. And then Byrhtnoth is pierced by 'a dart' (i.e. a spear). Wulfstan's son, described as 'not quite grown', is fighting beside his leader and pulls the spear from his body. Byrhtnoth draws his sword, but too late – one of the Vikings smashes his arm and his sword falls to the ground. He still urges his people on, but realises that he's dying and makes his peace with God. He's cut down by the Vikings, as are some of his loyal men. When Byrhtnoth dies, Godric flees the battlefield on Byrhtnoth's horse. Others, thinking that their leader is retreating, follow Godric. But some of Byrhtnoth's warriors fight on, including Dunnere, described as an 'unorne ceorl' (a simple churl, i.e. much lower in social status than most of the named warriors – who all boast about their lineage in the poem, in accordance with the convention of heroic Germanic poetry).

The text of the poem ends with even an aged retainer saying he will fight on to avenge his lord. In real life, the Vikings won the battle, and afterwards Byrhtnoth's body was found with his head missing and his gold-hilted sword in his body.

Some scholars interpret the poem as showing the sin of pride ('ofermode' – especially as the only other time the word is found in Anglo-Saxon poetry is to decribe Lucifer's actions); others take the view that Aethelred should have responded to the Vikings with battle rather than payment. This was a raiding party rather than an invasion party; so, if Byrhtnoth had kept the Vikings at bay or paid them off, they would probably have sailed up the coast and raided settlements there. As an ealdorman, Byrhtnoth had a duty to protect others, so he was forced to fight.

Statue of Byrhtnoth on the Promenade at Maldon.
Photograph by author.

After the battle, Archbishop Sigeric of Canterbury advised King Aethelred to buy off the Vikings rather than continue the armed struggle. The result was a payment of 10,000 Roman pounds (3,300 kg) of silver, the first example of Danegeld being paid in England.

The landscape back then was slightly different because the channel between mainland and Northey Island was much narrower; the sea level rose over the next few centuries and flooded the land, and then the land was reclaimed via the sea wall in the early 1800s. One archaeological survey has shown that the land surface of the tenth century is just over a metre and a quarter below the current sea marsh.

The battle is also mentioned in other records, including the *Anglo-Saxon Chronicles* (which began to be compiled in the ninth century and continued recording contemporary events until the 1150s), a treaty arranged by Archbishop Sigeric of Canterbury with Aelfric and Aethelweard (two of the main ealdormen), and the *Life of St Oswald of Worcester*, which was written in Ramsey Abbey between 997 and 1000.

The *Chronicle of Ely* also refers to the battle – understandably, because Byrhtnoth gave endowments to the abbey at Ely and was buried there. The chronicle says that Justin and Guthmund led the Viking forces; it also says that there was an earlier battle at Maldon in 987, when Byrhtnoth slew nearly all the Vikings on the bridge (i.e. the causeway) and the battle in 991 was the Vikings' attempt at vengeance.

According to the *Chronicle of Ely*, Byrhtnoth's body was buried in Ely with a ball of wax in place of his head. The eighteenth-century antiquarian James Bentham examined the bones in Byrhtnoth's resting-place and said that there was no head and the collarbone had clearly been cut in two by either an axe or a sword.

Spooks: the Maldon fairies

It's said that at twilight, you can see fairies walking on the marshes at Maldon.

Martello Towers

Martello towers were built along the south and east coast between Aldeburgh and Sussex between 1803 and 1812 to resist any attempted invasion by Napoleon.

The idea came during the war in Corsica, when the Royal Navy went to the aid of Corsican patriots against the French and bombarded the large round tower on Mortella Point. They'd already captured the tower in September 1793, when *HMS Lowestoft* bombarded it for two hours, but the Corsican patriots lost it to the French again. In February 1794, *HMS Fortitude* and *HMS Juno* sailed into Fiorenzo bay and attacked the tower; although

Martello tower at Clear Point, St Osyth
Photograph by author.

they were repulsed, the British Army had landed further up the coast, besieged the tower and took it. Vice-Admiral Hood later reported of the battle at sea:

> The Fortitude and Juno were ordered against it, without making the least impression by a continued cannonade of two hours and a half; and the former ship being very much damaged by red-hot shot, both hauled off. The walls of the Tower were of a prodigious thickness, and the parapet, where there were two eighteen-pounders, was lined with bass junk, five feet from the walls, and filled up with sand; and although it was cannoned from the Height for two days, within 150 yards, and appeared in a very shattered state, the enemy still held out; but a few hot shot setting fire to the bass, made them call for quarter. The number of men in the Tower were 33; only two were wounded, and those mortally.

The tower at Mortella was demolished before the British left in 1796, but the tower's defensive strength impressed Admiral Sir John Jervis, the Commander-in-Chief of the Mediterranean, who wrote that he 'hoped to see such works erected on every part of the [English] coast likely for an enemy to make a descent on.'

Thus the idea of Martello towers was born; the word was a corruption of 'Mortella', although there is also some confusion with the 'torre de martello' or hammer towers used on the Italian coast, where a hammer struck a bell to warn that pirates were approaching.

The east coast towers were built to stop Napoleon's armies marching on London from the east; because the east coast isn't quite as steep as the south coast, the Martello towers there are larger than those built on the south coast. They were mini forts, built from stone or rendered brick. The ground floor acted as the magazine and store room; the garrison (usually one officer and 24 men) lived on the first floor in a 'casemate', which was divided into several rooms and had fireplaces for cooking and heating; and on the roof cannon were mounted on pivots so they could be turned through 360 degrees. There was usually a well or cistern for fresh water, and some had a drainage system to refill the cistern with rainwater.

Around 29 towers were built between Aldeburgh in Suffolk and St Osyth in Essex; 18 of them survive, 6 of them in Essex. The towers were thicker at the front than at the back, and it's said that each tower took 700,000 bricks to build. The bricks were made at Grays in Essex and transferred by boat to the site of each tower.

They were never actually used during the Napoleonic Wars; after the threat from the French receded, some of the towers were demolished or swept away by coastal erosion, others were made into homes, and some were taken over by the coastguard and used to fight against smuggling. During the Second World War, some Martello towers acted as observation platforms.

The Towers of Essex

The towers in Essex were all designated with letters of the alphabet:

Tower A, at Point Clear in St Osyth's (OS Grid Reference TM 083156), is currently used as the East Essex Aviation Society Museum. It was the first of the towers to be built in 1810, and originally had a battery in front of it. During the Second World War, a minefield was laid at the entrance to the River Colne and the mines were controlled from this tower.

Tower B, nearby at Beacon Hill in St Osyth's (OS Grid Reference TM 095147), was sold by the war office and became a private home; it was also used as a radio astronomical observatory by Mr F. Hyde. It was demolished in 1967 and the site is now a housing development.

Tower C, at Jaywick (OS Grid Reference TM 136127), was sold by the War Office in 1906 and became a private home, before turning into a refreshment room and club. In the Second World War, it was occupied by the army. It is in the middle of a holiday camp and has been an arts centre since 2005. On the roof there is a look-out station for the National Coastwatch Institute.

Tower D, at Clacton (OS Grid Reference TM 161133), is now disused and stands on a golf course. Originally, the tower guarded a sluice which could be opened to flood the surrounding marshes.

Tower E, also at Clacton (OS Grid Reference TM 167137), was built in 1812 to command the 'landing place at Clacton Wash and the great road leading from it into the country'. It became part of Butlin's holiday camp in 1935 and has since been used as a water tower.

Tower F, at Marine Parade in Clacton (OS Grid Reference TM 173143), originally had a battery built in front of it, but this was apparently lost to coastal erosion in 1883. It's the only tower which still has its original drawbridge, and it also has a moat. The roof was used as a coastguard lookout from 1888, and in the First World War it was used as a station for the Essex Regiment. In 1931 it was used as a museum, then in the Second World War it was used by the Ministry of Defence. It has also been used as a meeting place for the Scouts, and a model village was built there in the 1970s. A couple of years ago it became a restaurant called 'Tower F', which has since closed.

Tower G, at Holland Haven (OS Grid Reference TM 219172), was built in 1810-12; the site was sold for auction in 1819, along with the sites of Towers H and I (making £2,675 in total), and was demolished shortly afterwards.

Tower H, at Holland Haven (OS Grid Reference TM 227181), was sited in the middle of present-day Frinton Golf Course and was built in 1810-12; the site was sold for auction in 1819, along with the sites of Towers G and I, and was demolished shortly afterwards. Its materials were used for farm buildings at Kirby. It was the only one of the Essex Martello towers not to have a battery.

Tower I, at Holland Haven (OS Grid Reference TM 235188), was built in 1810-12; the site was sold for auction in 1819, along with the sites of Towers G and H, and was demolished shortly afterwards.

Tower J, at Walton Cliffs (OS Grid Reference TM 253215), was built in 1810-12; the site was sold for auction in 1835. Because it was in a dangerous state, due to coastal erosion, it was demolished; years later, the ditch was turned into the Round Garden at Walton.

Tower K at Walton (OS Grid Reference TM 250220) was built to guard Walton Creek. It's in the middle of the Martello Caravan Park in Kirby Road and the tower is disused.

A report in the times from 11 February 1811 talks about one of the newly built towers:

> One of the Martello Towers on the coast of Essex near St Osyth, has given way. Its first inclination was several feet one way; in order to restore it to its situation, the ground was excavated on the other side, and it has not gone back with an inclination in nearly the same proportion the other way. What is very singular, though the fabric must have sustained a great deal of percussion, no crack or fissure appears in the brickwork.

❅ ❅ ❅

Mersea Priory

The church of St Peter and St Paul in West Mersea (OS map reference TM0091 1250) was probably originally established by Cedd and his months in the seventh century, on the site of Roman foundations. It was damaged by Norse raiders in 894 and then rebuilt. The church was described as a minster at the beginning of the tenth century, and was associated with the Benedictine priory set up by the abbey of St Ouen, which is thought to have been sited to the west of the church. There are some Saxon features in the church, as well as reused Roman materials, but most of the present church dates from the fourteenth century with parts rebuilt in the sixteenth century.

Tower of the church of St Peter and St Paul, West Mersea.

Photograph by author.

The Beginnings of the Priory

The priory was granted to the abbey of St Ouen at Rouen by Edward the Confessor in 1046. Little is known of the history of the priory; its court rolls (records of services, tithes, disputes and the like) were burned during the Uprising of 1381.

As an alien priory, Mersea was seized by the king several times in the thirteenth and fourteenth centuries, but in 1400 St Ouen abbey had licence from Henry IV to grant the priory and its belongings to John Doreward, his wife Isabel, and Henry, the bishop of Annaghdown. They had to maintain the buildings, keep holding divine services and keep all the liberties and customs.

The End of the Priory

Henry V dissolved all alien priories in 1415 and in 1422 granted the priory to the Archbishop of Canterbury for a college he was founding at Higham Ferrers. After Dissolution, in 1542, the site was granted to Robert Dacres.

Scandals: the Beached Whale

A whale was beached on the priory's lands in 1300 and there was a row between the bailiffs of Colchester, who wanted it for the king, and the prior, who seized it for his own use. A similar event occurred in 1381 and the sheriff was ordered to seize it for the king.

Danish Raiders & the Temporary Camp

The *Anglo-Saxon Chronicle* mentions that the Danes made a temporary camp on the island in 894. It has been suggested that the moated area of St Edmund's church at East Mersea (OS map reference TM 060150) may have enclosed a Danish encampment.

The church of St Edmund, King and Martyr, East Mersea.
Photograph by author.

Spooks: the Roman Centurion

The road onto Mersea Island (which has the Pyfleet channel on the east and the Strood channel on the west) is on a causeway known as the Strood. When mainland water was laid to the island in 1978, a number of wooden piles were found underneath the causeway. They were radio-carbon dated to between A.D. 684 and 702, making it the only known causeway in Britain that's datable to the seventh or eighth century. It's thought that the causeway originally consisted of between 15 and 20 rows of piles; each row was up to 500m long.

A Roman centurion has been seen by many drivers and pedestrians, marching from East Mersea across the causeway and along the road towards the little village of Peldon. The first to record the ghost was the Rev Sabine Baring-Gould of East Mersea, in 1904 (though, given that Baring-Gould was a novelist, it's quite possible that he made up the story!). Apparently, the centurion is most likely to be seen around the equinox, on 23 September.

There is a barrow next to the Strood, which is also known as Mersea Mount; it's thought to date from the first century AD. When it was excavated in 1912, a small burial chamber was found in the centre. It contained a lead box with a wooden lid, and inside the box was a green glass bowl containing cremated human remains. A spring of running water was also found a few inches below the foundation of the tomb

In 1969, Leslie Haines speculated that, although the barrow was a British barrow, the contents were Roman, so he believed that the barrow may have been built by a British chieftain for his Roman wife.

Spooks: the Danish leaders and the Buried Ship

The rector of East Mersea, Rev Sabine Baring-Gould, was also a novelist and tells the tale of Barrow Hill (Mersea Mount) in his novel *Mehalah*. In it, he says that when the Danes spent the winter on Mersea, their leaders were twins. One spring, they sailed to St Osyth, where they killed the saint (see page 31) but brought her beautiful sister back with them. They both fell in love with her and were jealous of each other, so they ended up fighting each other with swords to win her favour – but both died in the battle.

The Danes drew their ship to a hill just above the Strood and put the girl in the hold with one brother either side, then and buried them while she was still alive. And so the story goes, at the time of the new moon, the flesh starts to grow back on their bones. On nights with a full moon, you can hear the Danish twins screaming and fighting, but as the moon wanes their flesh drops away again and the screaming gradually grows quieter. When there is no moon, you can hear the woman crying until the new moon appears, and the cycle starts all over again.

However, Baring-Gould admitted that the tale was entirely fictional, and brings in several strands from various Germanic legends.

Spooks – the Buried Witch

At East Mersea, some people believe that a witch was buried in the churchyard –Sarah Wrench, who died aged 15 on 6 May 1848. So the legend goes, she's buried on the north (unconsecrated) side of the church, with an iron cage over her to stop her coming back to life and troubling the villagers. Other stories say that she wasn't a witch, but she had a child out of wedlock; this meant that the church disapproved of her and was the reason why she was buried on the north side.

It's obvious to modern eyes that the grave is covered by a mortsafe. Mortsafes were used earlier in the nineteenth century to protect the body of the deceased from being dug up by the 'resurrection men' and used for anatomical study by medical students. However, some questions remain unanswered. After the Anatomy Act of 1832 allowed medical schools to procure corpses for dissection from other sources than just hanged criminals, the 'resurrection' trade was no longer necessary. So why was her grave covered with a mortsafe, sixteen years after the Act was passed? And why is it the only one in the churchyard with a mortsafe?

Grave of Sarah Wrench, East Mersea. Photograph by author.

Mountfitchet Castle

Mountfitchet Castle (OS map reference TL5153 2500) is a reconstruction of the Norman stone ringwork and bailey fortress (i.e. there are two circles of land next to each other, forming a figure of eight, with a drawbridge connecting them). Originally the ringwork had a wet ditch round it, and the bailey had ramparts and ditches. It is open to the public from March to November.

The Beginnings of the Castle

The site is thought to have been an Iron Age fort; during excavations, items have been found to suggest that there were also settlements there in Roman, Saxon and Viking times.

The castle was founded by Robert Gernon, duke of Boulogne. Robert's son, William, changed his surname to Mountfitchet and also founded the abbey of Stratford Langthorne (see page 113); he enlarged the castle and built it in stone, pulled down his father's wooden fences and built a stone curtain wall.

William's great-grandson, Richard, was one of the 'disaffected barons' who rebelled against King John. At Runnymede, 15 June 1215, Richard Mountfitchet was chosen as one of the 25 barons who would enforce the Magna Carta. However, King John annulled the charter, with Pope Innocent III's help, and started the civil war.

Remains of a twelfth-century wall at Mountfitchet Castle. Photograph by author.

John's forces besieged the castles at Hedingham (see page 25) and Colchester (see page 48), and Richard fled back to Mountfitchet. John followed and attacked the castle – he breached the walls, slighted the castle, and set everything he could on fire.

In 1216, Richard's lands and titles were restored by Henry III, though the castle was not rebuilt. Much of the stone was removed by villagers to build their houses, but remains of the twelfth-century castle can be seen on the south slope. Richard had no children, so his three sisters were his heirs; eventually Mountfitchet became part of the De Vere lands.

The castle was reconstructed in 1984-6 as an earth and timber castle.

Ghosts

A one-armed knight – nicknamed 'Sidney' by the staff – has been seen in the Great Hall. In August 2008 a group of paranormal investigators held a vigil at the castle; although they didn't pick up the one-armed knight, they reported linking to a spirit who'd been arrested for theft and then hanged as a warning. They also picked up many deaths from the plague in 1368, took photographs of orbs and heard noises.

Remains of a twelfth-century gateway at Mountfitchet Castle. Photograph by author.

Ongar Castle

Ongar Castle (OS map reference TL5544 0309) is the remains of a twelfth-century motte and bailey castle. The centre of Chipping Ongar lies in the middle of the earthworks. The castle lies to the north-east of the high street; the mound is 50 feet high and 230 feet in diameter, and has a 12-foot moat all the way round it. It is on private land, but you can see it from the Essex Way footpath (just behind the library).

Part of the motte at Ongar Castle.
Photograph by author.

The Beginnings of the Castle

Some historians believe that the castle was built by Eustace, Count of Boulogne (Edward the Confessor's brother-in-law, who fought on the side of the Normans at Hastings and was one of the four men who killed Harold) as part of the Honour of Boulogne.

Ongar passed to King Stephen via his wife Maud, and their son William gave it to Richard de Lucy around 1153-4. Richard was later the justiciar to Henry II; he was the sheriff of Essex and was the king's representative when Henry II was in France. Richard may have been the one who built the castle; he then enlarged and strengthened it. The castle had some royal favour; Henry II visited in 1164 and Edward II visited in 1326.

The End of the Castle

The castle eventually became part of the Duke of Buckingham's estate. When Edward Stafford was executed for treason in 1521, the king seized the castle and rented it out. Eventually, it went to the Morris family. In 1647, John Morris was charged with forging documents (including Acts of Parliament) to secure titles to various manors, including Ongar, and the petitioners won their claims.

The castle was demolished in the sixteenth century and the owner of the land, William Morris, replaced it with a three-storey brick building in 1579. It fell into ruins and was demolished in 1744 by Edward Alexander; it was replaced by a summer house which also fell into ruins and wasn't replaced. An article in the *Gentleman's Magazine* 1808 says that a small portion of wall was still visible then.

Pleshey Castle

Pleshey Castle (OS map reference TL665 145) is the remains of an eleventh-century motte and bailey castle. The motte is one of the largest in England, 55 feet high and 295 feet across at the base, surrounded by a deep ditch and an outer bailey. It's located behind the church but you'll get a better view of the motte from the viewing-point in the centre of the village. The castle is on private land but is open to the public during heritage events and by appointment.

The Beginnings of the Castle

The castle may have been a Roman settlement to begin with as Roman bricks have been found there. After 1066 William granted the site to Geoffrey de Mandeville (who also owned Saffron Walden, see page 109), and Geoffrey built a wooden palisade or tower on the mound.

Civil war and treason

Geoffrey's grandson – also named Geoffrey de Mandeville – increased the height of the motte, built the ramparts and dug the moat, then rebuilt the castle in stone. He was the constable of the Tower of London and was originally on Stephen's side in the Civil War, but in 1141 he switched sides and Matilda made him Sheriff of Essex. When London wouldn't accept Matilda as the queen, Geoffrey switched sides again. Stephen pardoned him for supporting Matilda and gave him more lands,

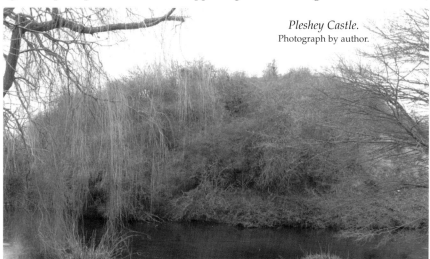

Pleshey Castle.
Photograph by author.

96

and also made him Sheriff of London and Middlesex. This meant that Geoffrey was very powerful and unsurprisingly Stephen felt threatened by him.

Geoffrey met Matilda in secret and supported her. When she lost her bid for the throne, Stephen – who'd been watching Geoffrey – accused him of treason, and made him surrender his castles and his titles. Geoffrey fled and hid in the fens in Cambridge, becoming the head of a band of outlaws. He attacked one of Stephen's outposts, was wounded in the head in the Siege of Burwell, and died in 1144.

Castle in the village sign, Pleshey. Photograph by author.

Because he'd been looting churches in his outlaw days, particularly Ramsey Abbey in Cambridgeshire, according to the eighteenth-century historian Philip Morant – he was excommunicated, which meant that he wasn't allowed to have a burial in church. Because of this, Geoffrey's body was kept unburied in a lead coffin in Temple Church for twenty years; other sources say that the coffin was hung on a crooked tree in the orchard. Eventually William, the first prior of Walden Abbey (see page 106) persuaded the pope to give Geoffrey absolution.

Henry II restored the estates and castles to Geoffrey's eldest son in 1156, but two years later had the castle at Pleshey dismantled and ordered the moat to be filled in. (Excavations have confirmed that the moat was filled in at that point.) However, Geoffrey's younger son, William, refortified the castle somewhere between 1167 and 1180. William redeemed himself in royal eyes because he went on crusade to Jerusalem, and carried the crown at the coronation of Richard I.

Raided by King John

Eventually the castle passed to the Fitzpiers family. Geoffrey Fitzpiers supported John, so when John became king he made Geoffrey the fourth Earl of Essex. Geoffrey's son, the fifth Earl, became one of the rebel barons. As a result, the castle was pillaged by Savaric de Mauléon, a troubadour and Poitevin noble who commanded some of John's mercenaries, the day before he went to Coggeshall (see page 124), and it was besieged by the Earl of Salisbury on behalf of John in 1216.

The Ambush of Thomas of Woodstock

Through marriage, the castle passed to Thomas of Woodstock, Duke of Gloucester. Richard II believed that Gloucester was intending to overthrow him, so he took decisive action in 1397. He visited the castle unexpectedly, and Gloucester brought his wife Eleanor and small children to greet the king before arranging for refreshments. Once the king had eaten, he asked Gloucester to saddle half a dozen horses and ride with him to London to meet with Dukes of York and Lancaster, because he wanted Gloucester's advice on their proposal.

Gloucester, suspecting nothing, did as he was asked. When they reached Stratford, Thomas Mowbray, the Earl Marshal, who had been lying in wait, apprehended him and said that Gloucester was under arrest for plotting against the king. Gloucester called to the king, thinking it was a mistake, but Richard simply ignored him and continued riding. Gloucester was taken to the Thames and put on a ship to Calais, where he was strangled (though at the time Richard tried to hush it up and claimed that Gloucester died of apoplexy).

Eleanor retreated to the nunnery at Barking (see page 12), and Pleshey started to slide into ruin. She eventually returned to Pleshey, where she died in October 1399.

The episode is highlighted in *Richard II* I, ii, in Eleanor's speech:

> *With all good speed at Pleshy visit me.*
> *Alack, and what shall good old York there see*
> *But empty lodgings and unfurnished walls,*
> *Unpeopled offices, untrodden stones.*
> *And what hear there for welcome but my groans.*

After her death, Richard promptly took the castle. When he died at Pontefract Castle and Bolingbroke was crowned as King Henry IV, Richard's followers fled. The Duke of Exeter (who was one of the men responsible for capturing Gloucester) fled from London, but Gloucester's men found him and took him to Pleshey Castle; they beheaded him and stuck his head on a pole.

The End of the Castle

Margaret d'Anjou lived at the castle in the 1450s and was responsible for building the brick bridge. A survey from 1558 says that the castle was in ruins but the bridge was still there along with various timber buildings including a hall, a constable's house, a kitchen and the outer gatehouse.

In 1629, Robert Clarke, pulled down the castle for building material to build a new house, The Lodge. Excavations in 1907 showed foundations of a stone building, which was either the keep or the Great Hall.

Spooks: Eleanor's Buried Treasure

Eleanor, the Duchess of Gloucester, supposedly had her treasure buried in the moat in a huge chest that nobody can drag up; according to legend, someone once tried to move the chest with horses, but the chains broke and the treasure chest sank back into the moat.

Prittlewell Priory

Prittlewell Priory (OS map reference TQ8771 8733) is the remains of a Cluniac monastery dedicated to St Mary. The remains consist of the priory refectory and the prior's chamber; the foundations of the priory church and other buildings are also visible on the site. The area is now used as the Priory Museum.

Prittlewell; plate from Thomas Kitson Cromwell's Excursions Through Essex, 1818-9.

The Beginnings of the Priory

The priory was founded as a cell to the Cluniac Priory of St Pancras at Lewes by Robert FitzSweyn, at some time between 1086 and 1121, and between twelve and eighteen monks lived at the priory. It became denizen (i.e. the monks paid the king a fee so the priory could become considered an English priory rather than an 'alien' one subject to higher taxes) between 1351 and 1374.

The End of the Priory

The priory was dissolved in 1536, by which time there were only seven monks left. The site was granted to Thomas Audley, and ten years later he sold it to Lord Rich. By this point, most of the buildings had been demolished, and the prior's lodging had become a farmhouse.

In 1917, Robert Jones bought the site and presented the buildings to the borough. Excavations have shown that there is an Iron Age site beneath the church, as well as a Saxon defended settlement and a burial ground.

Spooks

It's said that the priory is haunted by a monk, and local birds tend to be very fidgety when he appears. In one version of the story, he was involved in black magic; another version says that he fell in love with a local woman. Both may just be legends, but during an archaeological dig in the 1960s the grave of a disgraced monk was discovered.

Children are sometimes heard playing on the first floor of the museum, but when people go to investigate they find that the room is empty.

There's also a legend nearby at Prittlewell churchyard. Samuel Brown, who was buried in 1827, has been heard trying to escape from his coffin.

Scandals

William le Auvergnat, who was a monk from Lewes, became prior in 1311. Three years later, he was accused of incontinency (i.e. he'd been unchaste) in the city of London. The Cluniac visitation couldn't get the full facts of the story, so they ordered the Prior of Lewes to make an inquiry. The Prior of Lewes decided to deprive le Auvergnat of the priory, but then there was a huge fight over who should replace him. Lewes said that Guichard de Caro Loco should be the new prior; however, the king had appointed Prior William and refused to change that. In February 1316, the king sequestered the priory on the excuse of its poverty, and appointed Adam de Osgodeby to take custody.

In December 1316, the Prior of Lewes made James de Cusancia the Prior of Prittlewell, and there was a fight between James and William as to who should be prior; William entered the priory forcibly, backed by an armed mob, and in retaliation the Prior of Lewes sent out a warrant for his arrest as an apostate (i.e. saying that he'd renounced the religious life without permission)., in both 1317 and 1318.

In August 1318, William renounced his claim – but then he invaded the priory again, backed by an army as before, and appealed to the archbishop of Canterbury to help him. The Prior of Dunmow oversaw the case and ruled in William's favour. James promptly appealed to the archbishop and threw William out before the case could be heard. The archbishop's court ruled in favour of William, but James had no intention of giving up. He appealed again to the archbishop and the pope, and meanwhile the Prior of Lewes took matters into his own hands. He sent his men to the priory and, while William was celebrating mass, they wounded him in the

Prittlewell Priory. Photograph by author.

head, bound him and three other monks hand and foot, and took him to Lewes. William died in 1321 and James occupied the priory; he resigned in 1334 and later became the Prior of Thetford.

In 1431, another of the monks turned apostate – John de Raylegh (also known as John Hugh). He was in prison in London within three days of the writ being issued, and there was also a complaint on file by a London merchant. John was handed over to the sub-prior to be dealt with.

The Prittlewell Prince

Back in the 1880s, when the Liverpool Street to Southend railway line was being constructed, an Anglo-Saxon cemetery and Roman burials were discovered at Prittlewell. More evidence was found when Priory Crescent was built in 1923. However, the huge discovery didn't come until 2003, when archaeologists were excavating the area because proposals had been made to widen the A127 at Priory Crescent. They came across an unplundered Saxon burial which has since become known as the 'Prittlewell Prince' and is the most important Saxon burial discovered since Sutton Hoo in 1939.

Although the exact identity of the prince is unknown, we know that he was male (he was buried with a weapons rather than beads and brooches), and we know that he was of high status because the goods buried with him were expensive and point to wide trading links.

The man was buried in a wooden chamber that was four metres square by one and a half metres high, which was then covered over with a mound. As the roof decayed, the mound collapsed into the grave and covered the body and its contents. The acidic soil dissolved the body, but the belongings were still there and, in some cases, still hanging on the pegs of the walls of the room – exactly where they'd been placed on the day of the funeral.

More than 100 items were found, including those use for domestic purposes (bowls, flagons and cauldrons), entertainment (gaming pieces and gold-rimmed drinking horns, plus the first complete outline of an Anglo-Saxon lyre ever found in Britain), ceremony (an iron standard and a folding stool which is unique in Britain but is portrayed in early medieval images of kings), and religious items (two small gold crosses which may have been placed over his eyes, a silver spoon, a buckle that may have been a reliquary), plus gold coins.

The coins, buckle and blue and green glass jars found at the site dated from between 600 and 640, so it's possible that the burial was that of King Saebert of Essex, a pagan who converted to Christianity and helped St Mellitus set up St Paul's cathedral in London. Saebert died in 616 and his sons reverted to paganism, expelling the Christian missionaries.

The road scheme is going ahead using an alternative route, and the burial site will be preserved with a memorial erected.

Rayleigh Mount

Rayleigh Mount (OS map reference TQ8049 9095) is a motte and bailey castle overlooking the Crouch valley. Only the earthworks remain above ground. The site is managed by the National Trust and it is open to the public.

The Beginnings of the Castle

Rayleigh Mount is one of the few castles mentioned in Domesday, so it's one of the earliest Norman castles in England. It may have been built on the site of a Roman building, as Roman brick fragments have been found there. There is documentary evidence to show that the castle was occupied from 1070 to the mid-1300s.

Excavations in the middle of the twentieth century showed that there were several periods of construction. The first, from 1070-1135, was when the motte was constructed. The castle defences were complete between 1135 and 1163; the third period, 1163-1270, saw the defences being developed further. From 1270, part of the bailey was raised, and the fourth period, up to 1350, saw the bailey completely redeveloped.

The land belonged to Robert FitzWymarc. His son Swyen inherited it at the end of the eleventh century and he rebuilt it and strengthened it, adding vineyards and a hunting park; by 1140 the motte was faced in stone rubble. After Sweyn died, the castle passed to his son Robert de Essex, and then to Robert's son, Henry d'Essex.

Scandal: Henry d'Essex

Henry d'Essex was Henry II's standard bearer at the Battle of Counsylth (Coleshill) in 1157. Apparently, he heard several people cry, 'The King is slain!' – and in response he threw down the standard and fled the field in terror.

Henry II saw Essex's action as the result of fear rather than intentional desertion, and d'Essex continued as the royal constable; he also served in Toulouse in 1159. But Robert de Montfort (whose family had lost Haughley Castle in Suffolk to d'Essex) saw his chance to win his lands back and charged d'Essex with being a coward and a traitor. De Montfort made the point that Roger, the Earl of Clare, had rallied the troops and picked up the standard when Essex had failed. On 31 March 1163, Henry II presided over the Curia Regis at Windsor and de Montfort formerly appealed (accused) d'Essex of cowardice. As this was three years before Henry II reformed the law to allow trial by jury at the Assize of Clarendon, this meant that Essex would face trial by ordeal.

In Anglo Saxon England, trial by ordeal took one of four forms. The first was that the accused had to eat a cake of barley bread while a priest prayed; if he was guilty, his face would seize up and he wouldn't be able to chew or swallow. (This sounds innocuous – but the stress of the situation would cause a dry mouth, and

Rayleigh Mount. Photograph by author.

trying to eat something dry without any saliva to help you swallow it would indeed make you choke.)

The second was trial by immersion: with a cord round his waist, the accused would be lowered into a pool. If he sank, he was innocent; if he floated, he was guilty.

The third was trial by hot iron: water would be heated in a cauldron in the church, and a piece of iron or a stone would be dropped in the bottom. When the water was at boiling point, the accused had to put his arm into the cauldron and take out the iron or stone. His arm would then be wrapped in a clean cloth and sealed by church. After three days, the seal would broken, the bandage unwrapped and his skin inspected. If it was healed, he was innocent.

The fourth was trial by fire, which worked in a very similar way to trial by hot iron. An iron was placed on the fire during mass; at the end of mass, the accused had to take it in his bare hand and carry it for a distance equivalent to nine times the length of his foot. Then his arm would be wrapped as per the trial by hot iron, and his skin inspected in the same way.

After the Norman Conquest, a fifth ordeal was added: this was trial by combat. Whoever won the battle also won the case. By the mid-twelfth century, this was the most fashionable form of ordeal – and, in court, the case of de Montfort versus d'Essex would be settled by trial by combat.

They exchanged gloves as a symbol of faith that both would turn up, and also 'wads' (pledges from neighbours as surety that they would turn up). The king announced that battle would take place on 8 April at Reading; the battleground was at Fry's Island near the Abbey.

In trial by combat, the duelling ground was sixty feet square and the two combatants had a quarterstaff and a shield; combat had to start before noon and end before sunset, and both parties had to swear an oath that they weren't using witchcraft or sorcery. The battle only ended when one of the combatants was dead or disabled – or if they shouted 'craven', but that meant being outlawed.

Sources differ as to what happened next; some say that d'Essex lay on the ground and pretended to be dead before de Montfort could land his first blow, while others say that the fight took place and de Montfort beat him so badly that the king thought d'Essex was dead, and told the monks of Reading Abbey to bury him as a traitor.

However, when the monks carried him away, they discovered that he was still alive, and they nursed him back to health. As a traitor, d'Essex had forfeited his lands, and as a coward he should have forfeited his life; however, the king pardoned d'Essex on condition that he became a monk. He did so, and told his story to two monks from Bury St Edmund: Abbot Sampson and Jocelin de Brakelond.

D'Essex claimed that during the battle he'd seen a vision that paralysed him: St Edmund and the knight Gilbert de Cereville had both appeared next to Robert de Montfort. He said then that it was divine retribution: he'd cheated the abbey at Bury St Edmunds, because he'd tried a criminal in his court at Haughley for an offence committed within the abbey of St Edmund's grounds, and hadn't paid the abbey a fine. As for Gilbert: d'Essex's wife claimed that the knight had made advances to her, so d'Essex threw him in prison, put him in chains and slowly tortured him until he died. Except Gilbert was innocent: d'Essex's wife had made the advances and, when Gilbert spurned them, decided to get her revenge.

The End of the Castle

After the king confiscated d'Essex's castles, Rayleigh belonged to the crown and passed to Richard I. Alterations were made in 1172 and 1183-4, and in 1200 King John gave Rayleigh to Hubert de Burgh. De Burgh robbed the stone from Rayleigh and used it for building his castle at Hadleigh (see page 63. When he died, the castle reverted to the Crown again, and was used as pasture during the last quarter of the thirteenth century; Queen Eleanor founded a stud at Rayleigh in the late thirteenth century, which has been associated with the castle.

In 1394, Richard II gave permission for the people of Rayleigh to use the foundations of the castle as building material, so clearly by then the castle had gone. The land was used after that as a farmyard and for grazing sheep. A brick tower windmill was built in the outer bailey in 1809 and is the tallest in Essex.

Rayleigh Mount was excavated in 1909-10 and 1959-61, and Roman bricks and an Anglo-Saxon brooch have been found in the area. During excavations, rabbit bones were found and dated to 1070, making them some of the oldest known rabbit bones in the country.

The Lawless Court

According to Blount's *Fragmenta Antiquitatis* (1679), there was a 'Lawless Court' in Rayleigh which was held on 'the Wednesday morning next after Michaelmas'. The steward wrote with coal rather than with ink, no candles were allowed, and everyone in the court had to whisper. The manor also held a 'Little Lawless' court six months earlier in the year, just before dawn on the Monday after Easter Monday. The court was transferred to King's Hill in Rochford in the fifteenth century; according to Philip Morant, writing in the eighteenth century, the court was 'kept at King's-hill, half a mile north-east of the church in the yard of a house belonging to Mr Crips and afterwards Robert Hackshaw of London'.

The formal name of the court was the 'King's Court of the Manor of King's Hill' and, so the tradition goes, on the morning of the Wednesday after Michaelmas Day, the Lord of the Manor of King's Hill (in Rochford) was woken by a cock crowing and discovered a group of his tenants planning to murder him. He convicted them of treason – which meant their lands would be forfeit – but decided to be merciful and let them keep their lands, on condition they attended the court. They had to gather at midnight in the place where the plot was discovered, on the anniversary, and the lord's steward would whisper their names. Tenants who didn't answer would be fined double rent for every hour they failed to attend – and they had to wait until a cock had crowed three times until they were able to leave.

The court continued until the nineteenth century. According to historian Courtney Kenny, writing in 1905, by then most tenants paid double rent in the steward's office in the morning, and a local man was paid 5 shillings to crow like a cock when the court's business was concluded.

Saffron Walden – Walden Abbey

Walden Abbey (OS map reference TL5262 3815) is the remains of a Benedictine priory dedicated to St Mary and St James the Apostle.

The Beginnings of the Abbey – and the Unburied Earl

The abbey was founded by Geoffrey de Mandeville, earl of Essex, between 1139 and 1143. Geoffrey was also responsible for founding the castles at Pleshey (see page 96) and Saffron Walden (see page 109). He switched sides several times in the civil war between Stephen and Matilda, and was eventually accused of treason and had to surrender his estates. He became an outlaw and was excommunicated for looting churches; so when he died in 1144 this meant that he wasn't allowed to be buried. As he was a Templar, his body was placed in a lead coffin, taken to London and kept within the Templar grounds.

In 1163, William, the first prior of Walden, persuaded the Pope to give Geoffrey absolution; however, when he went to claim Geoffrey's body from the Templars so that he could bury it in the place reserved for the founder of Walden church, he discovered that the

Audley End; plate from Thomas Kitson Cromwell's Excursions Through Essex, *1818-9.*

Templars had already buried Geoffrey secretly in their new cemetery.

Geoffrey's son (also named Geoffrey) was buried at Walden. His brother William succeeded to the title and complained about the amount his brother had given to the church. However, then William went on a pilgrimage to the Holy Land with Prior Reginald and became reconciled with him; after this, he granted more lands and goods to the monks at Walden. According to the eighteenth-century historian Philip Morant, William died at Rouen and was buried there, but his heart was brought back and buried at Walden Abbey.

Becoming an Abbey

The priory became an abbey on 1 August 1190 under the order of Richard I, and the king became the patron of the abbey. William's successor, Geoffrey Fitzpeter (who later became the Earl of Essex) said the monks had disinherited him and refused to

Audley End. Photograph by author.

give them what William had granted; the monks recorded that he took some of their sheep and put them inside the bailey walls of Walden Castle, and then did the same with more sheep and oxen. Then, rather nastily, once the sheep had died, he stuck them on top of the walls of the castle!

However, eventually he made it up with the monks and King John confirmed Geoffrey as the patron of the abbey.

Scandal: Neglect

In 1217, three of the monks complained to the bishop that the abbot neglected them and had ruined the abbey; the abbot of Westminster and the priors of Stoke and Hatfield Peverel were sent to make a visitation and fix the problem.

Scandal: Row between Archbishop and Bishop

In July 1281, there was a row between Archbishop Peckham and the bishop of London over a visitation that the bishop had made. Peckham wrote to the bishop, saying that he'd completely upset Peckham's arrangements: he'd disciplined the monks that Peckham thought worthy, let off the ones that Peckham had put in strict constraint, and appointed a prior that Peckham said was 'an enemy to religion'. To make it clear how unhappy he was, the archbishop ordered the bishop to give a copy of his work at the abbey to the bearer of the letter, to go straight back to Peckham.

Clearly there were some problems with discipline, because the Archbishop of Canterbury gave injunctions after his visitation in 1304 that the monks had to keep silent, keep their beds open and take their meals in the refectory (which had to be supplied with proper food). The monks were to be bled three days a week, and if they went outside the precincts they had to have a companion with them. They also had to give an annual statement of accounts, give the remnants of their meals to the poor, and give up their old clothes when new ones were given to them.

The End of the Abbey and the Married Abbot

Robert Baryngton, the abbot at Walden, took the Oath of Supremacy in 1534. However, there was a scandal because he admitted to Legh and ap Rice, the king's visitors, that he'd secretly got married. He was removed and the house was granted temporarily to William More.

The abbey was dissolved in 1538 and the site was granted to Sir Thomas Audeley.

Audley End and Excavations

It's said that many foundations of the abbey lie beneath the eastern lawn and flower beds of the house at Audley End. Excavations in1979 showed that the inner court of the house was the same size as the abbey cloister. Early finds made close by include several burials, iron nails (which archaeologists believe are evidence for wooden coffins), and two lead coffins; these were all probably from the monks' cemetery. Some human remains from a lay cemetery were also found, along with two circular bronze brooches with bronze swivel pins, dating from the thirteenth to the fourteenth century.

✤ ✤ ✤

Saffron Walden - Walden Castle

Walden Castle (OS map reference TL 5392 3871) is the stone remains of a twelfth-century keep. The area around the castle is open to the public, though the castle itself is fenced off.

The Beginnings of the Castle

Before the Norman Conquest, the lands were held by Ansgar, the king's standard bearer. When he died, his lands in Essex were given to Geoffrey de Mandeville I, the first constable of the Tower of London. His grandson (Geoffrey de Mandeville II) founded the castle as a motte and bailey fortress at some time around 1125, and in 1141 he was given permission by Empress Maud to move the market from Newport to the castle at Walden.

Saffron Walden Castle; plate from Thomas Kitson Cromwell's Excursions Through Essex, *1818-9.*

The castle was surrendered to King Stephen in 1142; he put it in the care of Turgis d'Avranches until 1145, and then it was possibly looked after by Reginald fitz Count. It was given back to Geoffrey's son Geoffrey III in 1156 but was slighted in 1157-8 (at a cost of £9 12s and 4d). It may have been refortified by William de Mandeville, Geoffrey III's younger brother, at some point between 1167 and 1180.

Scandals: Murder by Lance

In 1252 there was a tournament at the castle. One of the knights, Roger de Leiburne, had broken his leg in an earlier tournament and blamed his opponent. In revenge, he took the socket off his lance when he jousted with Ernauld de Montenei – and the lance went straight through de Montenei's throat.

The End of the Castle

In 1347 Humphrey de Bohun was given a licence to crenellate, though this probably refers to a stone house within the bailey rather than the old keep. The keep was later used as a semaphore station, a barn and a lime kiln. During the fourteenth century, the vats belonging to the dyers of the town were placed in the castle bailey ditches.

Spooks: the Cockatrice

There is a legend that a cockatrice lived near the town and was defeated by a man wearing mirrored armour. Folklore experts Jennifer Westwood and Jacqueline Simpson say the tale is likely to be the work of Robin Winstanley, a man who lived in Saffron Walden and compiled the annual *Poor Robin's Almanac*.

According to the legend, the cockatrice was tiny, only 30 cm tall; it was yellow-black, with red eyes and a white spot like a crown on its head. Nothing could grow where it lived because its breath was hot enough to roast plants; it also killed people with a look. According to Pliny, a cockatrice (which he knew by the name of 'basilisk') had a serpent's head and tail and the feet and wings of a cockerel, because it was hatched from a cockerel's egg by a toad or snake.

In King Street, Covent Garden, there was once a pub sign, the 'Essex Serpent', which related the cockatrice story.

A pamphlet dating from 1669, 'The Flying Serpent at Walden in Essex', gives a more detailed description of what happened to the cockatrice:

a most venomous serpent, which in former times lurked about the meads near Saffron Walden, who by his very sight killed so many, as the town became almost depopulated, when a valorous Knight, making him a coat of Christal glass, boldly went to assail this Cockatrice, but her venomous nature not being able to indure the

Saffron Walden Castle. Photograph by author.

110

purity of that fine mettle, she suddenly dyed, in memory whereof his sword was hung up in Walden Church, the effigies of the Cockatrice set up in Brass, and a Table hanged close by wherein was contained all the story of the adventure; but in these late times of Rebellion, it being taken for a monument of superstition was by the lawless soldiers broken in pieces, to shew they were also of a venomous nature as well as the Cockatrice.

Spooks: the Dragon

In 1699, Saffron Walden was apparently attacked again by another 'serpent'. This time, the beast was much larger: 9 feet long, with 'huge lustrous eyes, its teeth white and sharp'. It was apparently seen by the overseer of the poor and the churchwarden, as well as four householders, and sunned itself on the bank 'in a pasture ground near to a wood called Birchwood'. Eventually it went back into the wood, and although various people from the town waited for it with muskets, it wasn't seen again.

Spooks: Haunted Inns

The Cross Keys, on the corner of King Street and High Street, is allegedly haunted around midnight on 24 December, when footsteps can be heard marching up and down a passageway. It's said that the footsteps belong to a Cromwellian solder. Another Cromwellian soldier is alleged to haunt the Old Sun Inn, banging on the walls and moving furniture about.

Stanesgate Priory

Stanesgate Priory (OS map reference TL9309 0573) is the remains of a Cluniac priory dedicated to St Mary Magdalen. There are no visible remains. The site is privately owned and there is no public access.

The Beginnings of the Priory

Stanesgate Priory was founded between 1086 and 1121 as a cell to the Priory of Lewes by Ralph, the son of Brien (who held the manor at Domesday).

In 1293, the church was in near-ruinous condition, and the Prior of Lewes was ordered to make the prior of Stanesgate repair it. Clearly this didn't happen, because the order was repeated again in 1306, and it was stated that the house was 'spiritually and temporally in ruins.'

In the fourteenth century, being an alien priory, Stanesgate was seized several times by the king. The priory was so poor that the king actually let it off its arrears. In 1373, it became denizen (i.e. it paid a fee to the king so that it would be considered an English rather than an alien house and therefore have to pay less tax).

The End of the Priory

The priory was dissolved in 1525 and the revenues were granted to Cardinal Wolsey for his college – firstly at Oxford and then at Ipswich. After Wolsey fell from grace, the site was granted to the Hospital of St John of Jerusalem, and when that institution was dissolved in 1544 the site was sold to Edmund Mordaunt.

Spooks: the Devil and the Plough

According to local legend, a farmer was ploughing the field next to the old priory one day and was thoroughly fed up with the job; he said out loud that the devil could have his soul if he would do the ploughing. The Devil duly appeared and took the plough.

The farmer was terrified and ran to the priory church, with the devil following him. As the farmer went through the church door, the devil made a grab for him and just missed him – but, according to legend, the marks of his hand could be seen on the stone for many years.

✳ ✳ ✳

Stratford Langthorne Abbey

Stratford Langthorne abbey (OS map reference TQ 3902 8341) was also known as Stratford-atte-Bowe and West Ham Abbey; it was dedicated to St Mary and was one of the largest Cistercian abbeys in the country, owning 1,500 acres of land locally.

The abbey precinct was a site of about 8 hectares, between the Channelsea River on the west and Marsh Lane (Manor Road) on the east. Nowadays, the only remains are a keystone which is believed to be from the charnel house, which is set in to the tower wall in West Ham parish church. Abbey Mills Pumping Station is built on the site.

Chaucer mentions the abbey in the Prologue to the Canterbury Tales, when he introduces the prioress (rather neatly showing up her pretensions):

> And Frenssh she spak ful faire and fetisly
> After the scole of Stratford-atte-Bowe,
> For Frenssh of Parys was to hir unknowe.
> [And French she spoke fairly and fluently,
> After the school of Stratford-at-Bow,
> For the French of Paris she didn't know.]

The Beginnings of the Abbey

The abbey was founded by William de Montfichet in 1135 as a cell to Savigny Abbey in France. In 1218 it was hugely burdened by visitors, and the General Chapter ruled that Cistercian visitors on their way to London could only stay at the abbey for three days. Later, this was amended to say that visitors could stay for longer, as long as they fed their own horses and provided their own drink.

The Second Barons' War

In 1267, Henry III and his retainers came to Stratford Abbey. The king used the abbey as his court for the

Entrance to Stratford Abbey; plate from Thomas Kitson Cromwell's Excursions Through Essex, *1818-9.*

visitation of the papal legate, and made peace with the barons there after the Siege of London.

The Uprising of 1381

During the uprising of 1381, the abbey was looted and good were removed; charters were also burned.

Scandal: Bow Bridge

Bow Bridge was built in 1177; so the story goes, Maud, Henry I's queen, donated money to build the stone bridge at the spot after she'd 'been well washed in the water'. Originally, it was the responsibility of Barking to maintain the bridge, but then the responsibility passed to Stratford. There were several rows over the obligation, but eventually it was settled in 1315 that Stratford would maintain the bridge and the highway, and Barking would pay them £200 a year. After Dissolution there were similar rows over who was responsible for the maintenance of the bridge, which weren't settled until the Turnpike Trust was formed in 1834.

Keystone believed to be from charnel house in Stratford Langthorne Abbey, now set in the tower wall in West Ham parish church. Photograph by author.

Major Floods

The abbey was responsible for the sea walls around the marsh of West Ham. There was severe flood damage in the area at the end of the fourteenth century, and the monks had to move to Great Burstead (near Billericay). Richard II became the abbey's patron and restored it.

The End of the Abbey

The abbey was dissolved in 1538; the site was granted to Sir Peter Meautas and Johanna his wife. He let the buildings fall into ruin, and they were subsequently demolished. By the end of the eighteenth century, all traces of the buildings had gone, and the foundations had been dug out and used as building materials.

Excavations

The Woolwich Railway was built on the site in the 1840s. During construction in 1845, the workmen found a chamber. According to the newspaper report, it was

> *of oblong shape, rounded at one end and square at the other; about 12 feet long, 8 feet wide, and 5 feet in depth. The outer wall, which is of strong masonry, is about 6 inches thick; within that is a layer of cement, which is again lined with thin red tiles, of peculiarly close texture, and over these a thinner stratum of cement. These sides are (or rather were, for the greater part has been taken away by curiosity) neatly lined throughout with Dutch tiles, finely glazed, similar to those seen in old fashioned fire-places, but without the designs, being of a pure white.*

Because there was a well within two feet of the chamber, archaeologists believed that it was probably a lavatory. Excavations on the site located a lime kiln, lead-smelting pit, chapel and gatehouse, plus what archaeologists thought might be a keystone from the charnel house (as it was found near human remains); the stone block was decorated with carved skulls in a frame.

When the Jubilee Line extension was built, archaeological investigations took place between 1973 and 1994. Around 674 burials were excavated; some were reburied at Sutton Coldfield (where there is a Cistercian abbey) and a garden is planned for the site (subject to funding). The burials are interesting; only one child was found, buried in a wicker basket. A priest was found with a pewter chalice, and another body with a copper poultice dish. Many of the bones contained high levels of vitamin A, though it's not known why.

Spooks: William and the Lost Souls

So the legend goes, William, the cellerar of Stratford, was about to die when he heard a loud crack on the roof of the infirmary and the whole building shook. When his fellow monks came to see what the noise was, he told them that it was the arrival of all the souls he hadn't prayed for (because he was either negligent or too busy with his duties), demanding that he prayed for them now…

Thoby Priory

Thoby Priory (OS map reference TQ6263 9872) is the remains of an Augustinian monastery dedicated to St Mary and St Leonard. The structural remains consist of the part of the south wall of the presbytery. A house was built on the site but it burned down in the nineteenth century and there are no remains. The site is now a scrapyard and there is no access to the public.

The Beginnings of the Priory

It's unsure who founded the priory, but it's possible that Michael Capra, his wife Rose and his son William were the founders, as they granted a charter to Tobias the priest in 1141-51. The original name of the priory was Ginges; this changed to Gingetobye, then finally Thoby (probably from the first prior's name).

Scandals

At the Augustinian Chapter of 1443, Thoby was fined £1 (the equivalent of almost £500 in modern terms) for not sending representatives to the chapter.

Thoby Priory; plate from Thomas Kitson Cromwell's
Excursions Through Essex, *1818-9.*

The End of the Priory

As it was one of the smaller houses, the priory was suppressed in 1525 and the revenues were granted to Wolsey's college at Oxford. The prior had just died, and the two canons were transferred elsewhere. After Wolsey's fall from grace, the site was granted to Sir Richard Page, and after Page's death to William Berners.

Excavations

According to Duffield William Coller (writing in 1861), interesting things discovered during excavations include part of the figure of a Knight Templar, plus six coffins formed from tree trunks, scooped out and charred (two were opened and contained female skeletons). Knives with ivory handles were also found, along with coins and floor tiles.

In 1934, a timber coffin containing a skeleton was found near the priory wall; excavations in 2002 revealed 29 further graves.

Tunnels

According to legend, there's meant to be a tunnel between Thoby Priory and Ingatestone Hall – both sites were owned at one point by William Petrie. However, there's no evidence of a tunnel nowadays, and most of the alleged tunnels at monastic sites turn out to be simple drainage culverts.

Thremhall Priory

Thremhall priory (OS map reference TL531 214) was an Augustinian monastery dedicated to St James. Philip Morant, writing in 1769, says that it was built on the edge of Hatfield Forest, about two miles south-south-east from the church at Thremhall. Back then, the only part left of the priory was 'a garden wall on the north side of Mr Ray's house'; now the only remains are a moat and a fishpond.

The Beginnings of the Priory

The beginnings of the priory are slightly obscure. It's thought that it was founded by either Gilbert de Mountfitchet, just before he left for the Holy Land, or by his son Richard in 1150. Gilbert was said to have given the land to a Scot called Daniel so he could build the priory there, and Richard had a charter giving them a grant. Originally, the priory was for between five and six canons.

The End of the Priory

The priory was dissolved in 1536 and the site was granted to John Cary and Joice Walsingham. A house was built on the site in the eighteenth century, but has since been demolished.

Tunnels

There is supposed to be a tunnel leading from Birchanger to Thremhall Priory. However, there's no evidence of a tunnel nowadays, and most of the alleged tunnels at monastic sites turn out to be simple drainage culverts.

Scandal: marriage and denial

Around 1200, there was a scandal when Agnes Parage tried to prove that she married Arnold of Thorley, and his brother denied it. Agnes had lived with him for a long time before marriage and had had children with him. Witnesses said that the marriage had happened at the west door of the church in Thremhall, in the summer, with the prior wearing vestments. According to the witnesses, the marriage had followed the legal format: Arnold had put a ring on her finger with the words 'With this ring I wed you and with my body I honour you', a penny had been put on a book, and he'd given Agnes a third of his lands as dower. Agnes's father, brother and stepbrother had attended the marriage, but none of Arnold's family was there – he'd said that he didn't want his family there because they hated Agnes.

Tilbury Fort

Tilbury Fort (OS map reference TQ6509 7551) is the remains of a seventeenth-century fort overlooking the Thames. It is in the care of English Heritage and is open to the public.

The first permanent fort at Tilbury was a blockhouse built in 1539 by Henry VIII in response to the threat of a French invasion – the idea was to stop hostile ships attacking any of the towns on the coast, stop them from getting up the Thames to London, and stop soldiers disembarking from enemy ships. The blockhouse also guarded

Remains of Tilbury Fort; plate from Thomas Kitson Cromwell's Excursions Through Essex, *1818-9.*

the ferry crossing between Tilbury and Gravesend. It was known as 'Thermitage Bulwark', because it was on the site of a hermitage that had been dissolved in 1536.

The blockhouse was disarmed in 1553 and were in a poor condition by the time Elizabeth I was crowned in 1558.

Tilbury Fort and the Spanish Armada

In 1588, Philip II of Spain sent out a fleet to join an army in the Netherlands with the aim of invading England. The English fleet sailed to fight the galleons, and meanwhile Elizabeth I ordered emergency repairs to the fort and raised an army called the 'Citizen Militia', which gathered at West Tilbury, waiting until they were needed to repel the Spanish attack on London if the Armada managed to get control of the channel. On 9 August, Elizabeth came to rally her troops at Tilbury, wearing a breastplate and holding a sword, telling them:

My loving people, we have been persuaded by some, that are careful of our safety, to take heed how we commit ourselves to armed multitudes, for fear of treachery; but I assure you, I do not desire to live to distrust my faithful and loving people. Let tyrants fear; I have always so behaved myself that, under God, I have placed my chiefest strength and safeguard in the loyal hearts and good will of my subjects.

And therefore I am come amongst you at this time, not as for my recreation or sport, but being resolved, in the midst and heat of the battle, to live or die amongst you all;

to lay down, for my God, and for my kingdom, and for my people, my honour and my blood, even the dust.

I know I have but the body of a weak and feeble woman; but I have the heart and stomach of a king, and of a king of England, too; and think foul scorn that Parma or Spain, or any prince of Europe, should dare to invade the borders of my realms: to which, rather than any dishonour should grow by me, I myself will take up arms; I myself will be your general, judge, and rewarder of every one of your virtues in the field.

I know already, by your forwardness, that you have deserved rewards and crowns; and we do assure you, on the word of a prince, they shall be duly paid you. In the mean my lieutenant general shall be in my stead, than whom never prince commanded a more noble and worthy subject; not doubting by your obedience to my general, by your concord in the camp, and by your valour in the field, we shall shortly have a famous victory over the enemies of my God, of my kingdom, and of my people.

Although news reached Tilbury a few days later that the Armada had been beaten, the army wasn't disbanded until 17 August. However, after the treat had passed, the earthworks weren't maintained, and they had disappeared by the middle of the seventeenth century.

Tilbury Fort in the Civil War

Tilbury Fort was controlled by the City Militia as part of the Parliamentary defences during the English Civil War. In 1651 it was garrisoned by a governor, a lieutenant, an ensign, four corporals, one drummer, a master gunner, 16 matrosses (gunner's mates) and 44 soldiers.

After the Restoration, Charles II decided to upgrade the defences at Tilbury. Sir Bernard de Gomme, Charles II's chief engineer, submitted designs for a square fort, but no work was carried out. However, in 1667, when a Dutch naval squadron sailed up the Thames without being challenged, and then sailed on the Medway and burned part of the English fleet at Chatham, money was found for new forts. In 1670 de Gomme submitted a design for a pentagonal fort with five bastions; Charles II approved it and work began in September 1670.

The Water Gate at Tilbury Fort.
Photograph by author.

Work proceeded slowly, despite having a team of 265 craftsmen and workmen; it took almost fifteen years for the fort to be constructed, including levelling the old fort, cutting new ditches, raising new ramparts (as well as the centre of the fort, to avoid floods) and driving timber piles in the marsh to act as foundations for the building. The Water Gate (which was to be the main entrance to the fort) was completed in 1682.

Scandal: the Jacobite Prison

In 1745-6, Bonnie Prince Charlie led the Jacobite rebellion, which intended to restore the English and Scottish thrones to a descendant of James II, who had been deposed in 1688. The rebellion ended in a defeat at the Battle of Culloden in 1746. Of the 3,500 prisoners taken at the battle, 303 were sent by ship from Inverness to Tilbury. The conditions were dreadful and the prisoners were kept short of food. Just over 10% of them died of starvation or disease on the way. On 11 August 1746, the 268 survivors were imprisoned in the power magazines at Tilbury. Typhus killed 45 of them in the first month; and then it was decided that 1 in every 20 should stand trial for their life in 1747, so they had to draw lots to choose who was going to stand trial. The remainder stayed at the fort until their fate was decided; many of them were transported to Barbados and Antigua, and a very few were released. During the four years that the prisoners were kept there, tourists from London paid 6d for a place on the Westminster to Gravesend boat to see the dangerous prisoners. Some were even escorted into the magazines to look at the prisoners.

Scandal: the Cricket Match

According to the *London Chronicle* of 29 October, 1776, there was a cricket match in 1776 at the fort, between men of Essex and Kent. But when the Kent side brought in a ringer to play, the Essex men refused to play – and a fight started. When the Kentish men realised they were losing, one of them went into the guard house, grabbed a gun and shot one of the Essex cricketers dead. A full-scale riot ensued. According to the report, 'An old invalid was run through the body with a bayonet: and a serjeant who commands at the fort, in the absence of the officer, endeavouring with his four men to quell them, was shot dead.' Finally, the Essex men ran over the drawbridge and the Kentish men rowed away.

The End of the Fort

Tilbury became a second line of defence when a new fort was built at Coalhouse Point in the 1860s; but by the end of the century the weaponry was obsolete. During the First World War, Tilbury was used as a barracks for soldiers on their way to France and also became an Ordnance Depot. By 1925, it was decided that the fort was no longer useful, but attempts to sell it failed. During the Second World War, it was used as an anti-aircraft operations room until a purpose-built one opened at Vange in 1940. In 1950, the fort was demobilised and taken into care by the Ministry of Works. It was restored in the 1970s and opened to the public in 1982, and has been looked after by English Heritage since 1983.

Spooks: Captain Kidd the Pirate

One of the most notorious pirates was gibbeted at Tilbury.

William Kidd served on a 20-gun brig in St Kitts in 1689. He, Robert Culliford and his crewmates absconded with the ship to the English island of Nevis, rechristened the ship the *Blessed William*, and Kidd became the captain. They attacked various French settlements during King William's War (aka the War of the League of Augsberg). Kidd was rewarded with prize money (i.e. a share of the rewards of whatever he captured), but didn't share it with the crew. When he spent the night ashore, his crew stole the boat and his prize money, and sailed for New York.

A French governor was sympathetic and gave him a boat, the *Antigua*. Kidd tried to hunt down his boat but lost the trail; however, he settled in New York and married a wealthy widow in 1691. Four years later, he set sail for England, hoping to be given an officer's commission in the Royal Navy or to be given the command of a privateer (not quite a pirate vessel – privateers only attacked ships they believed to be hostile to their country). He was unsuccessful, but his friend Robert Livingston introduced him to Richard Coote, the Earl of Bellomont, who was an MP and the governor of Massachusetts. Bellomont was responsible for stopping piracy and smuggling, and asked Kidd to become a privateer. Kidd duly had a letter of commission from King William to be a privateer on the *Adventure Galley*. They were only to take treasure from pirates and not the ships of allies; the king would get 10% of the treasure, and of the remaining 90% Kidd and Livingston would get 15%, Bellomont and his backers 60% and the crew 25%. And if he didn't return with the booty within a year, he owed Bellomont and the backers £20,000 (the equivalent of around £2.25 million in modern terms).

Nine months later, they had still won no prizes – and the crew rebelled. Kidd stopped Captain Thomas Parker's ship but, while he was in discussion with Parker, his men ransacked Parker's ship. As soon as Kidd discovered this, he made his men return the stolen property. He also refused to let his men attack a Dutch ship because it was against the terms of his commission. William Moore, the gunner, claimed that Kidd had brought them to ruin. Kidd lost his temper and hit him with a bucket, fracturing his skull; Moore died the following day. The men were near mutiny, but then Kidd captured a French ship. A few months later, he captured the *Quedah Merchant*, netting an incredible £50,000-worth of cargo as well as treasure. He sold the opium and silk from the ship for £10,000 in gold bars, then headed for Madagascar – with his leaking ship bound together with ropes.

But then he met up with Robert Culliford, who had led the mutineers on the *Blessed William*. More than 100 of his crew decided to join Culliford and demanded their share of the prizes. Kidd was left with a useless ship, eleven loyal men and four cabin boys. He beached the ship, burned it, and set sail for the West Indies on the *Quedah Merchant*; on arrival at Anguilla in March 1699 Kidd learned that he'd been declared a pirate. Wanting to clear his name, he hid the ship, bought a sloop and then sailed to New York, where he met in secret with his wife and lawyer. His lawyer, James Emmott, met with Bellomont and handed over the passes from the French ships to prove that Kidd wasn't a pirate. Bellomont said that a pardon 'is possible' but refused to give Kidd the guarantee he wanted.

Kidd didn't entirely trust Bellomont, so he hid some of the treasure and then went to Boston with a detailed narrative of his voyage and the names of all the crew and mutineers. Bellomont had him arrested and put in jail. Kidd tried to escape, and was clapped in irons in Stone Prison, then shipped to London aboard the HMS *Advice*, still in chains. In London, he was questioned for seven hours and put in solitary confinement in Newgate Prison. Almost a year later, he testified in front of the House of Commons – and was still accused of being a pirate.

There were several trials; he was accused of murdering William Moore, and then of being a pirate and robber – including taking ships, torturing their crew and passengers, executing a native who had been tied to a tree, firing on English ships and kidnapping an English captain. All four juries returned a verdict of 'guilty'. When the judge asked what he had to say for himself, Kidd replied, 'I have nothing to say, but that I have been sworn against by perjured and wicked people.' The judge promptly sentenced him to execution.

The execution was set for 23 May 1701. Kidd was taken to the Execution Dock at Wapping and fed large quantities of rum before he was hanged – but then the rope broke. He fell to the ground, and was hanged a second time. This time, his body was chained to a post on the shore and left there for three tides, and then his corpse was put in an iron gibbet and hung at Tilbury Point (thought to be somewhere near Coalhouse Fort) for two years. His corpse was coated with tar to preserve it and stop the weather or pecking birds from making it deteriorate; and he would have been visible to ships as a warning not to turn to piracy.

So was Kidd a pirate? Maybe; maybe not. The French passes from the ships he captured that might have cleared his name disappeared before the trial (but were found in 1911 in the Public Records Office), and it's claimed that evidence was concealed for two of the trials.

And as for his famous treasure; rumour had it that the jewels on his ship were worth £30,000 (the equivalent of more than £3 million in modern terms) – but the items recovered from his ship were worth only about a fifth of that. Treasure hunters have looked for the fabled 'treasure island' where he hid the booty for hundreds of years, but it's never been found. His story has, however, inspired several authors, including Robert Louis Stevenson's *Treasure Island* and Edgar Allen Poe's short story 'The Gold Bug'.

Tilty Abbey

Tilty Abbey (OS map reference TL 6002 2666) is the remains of a Cistercian abbey dedicated to St Mary. The remains are used as the parish church; it was originally the chapel of the abbey gatehouse, dedicated to St Thomas of Canterbury. Because the chapel was outside the abbey precincts, it's unusual in that women could use the chapel as well as men.

Tilty Abbey; plate from Thomas Kitson Cromwell's Excursions Through Essex, *1818-9.*

The Beginnings of the Abbey

The abbey was founded by Robert de Ferrers, the Earl of Derby, and Maurice FitzGeoffrey in 1153. The earliest reference to the abbey is in Ralph of Coggeshall's chronicle, which says that the abbey was founded in 1153. The Louth Park Chronicle says that Tilty was a cell to the abbey of Warden in Bedfordshire, which was itself a cell of Rievaulx Abbey in Yorkshire. The Dunmow Chronicle says that the building of church was begun by Abbot Simon on 16 March 1188, and it was consecrated in 1221. As Cistercian abbeys followed a fairly set architectural pattern, Tilty probably looked quite similar to Tintern Abbey.

Plunder on Christmas Day

Tilty Abbey was pillaged by King John's army on Christmas Day 1215. Ralph de Coggeshall says that the soldiers broke in during mass, overthrew the furniture, broke open chests, and carried off booty. Ralph blamed the destruction on John's retainers, especially the Duc de Brabant (who then did the exactly the same to Coggeshall a week later (see page 40), then to the abbeys at Bury St Edmunds and Ely). Other sources say that the plundering was done by Savaric de Mauléon, a troubadour and Poitevin

Tilty Abbey gatehouse chapel.
Photograph by author.

*Arms of Tilty Abbey from
stained glass window in the church.*
Photograph by author.

noble who commanded some of John's mercenaries. Two coffin lids displayed on the north wall of the chancel in the church are thought to belong to the graves of two people who were killed in the riot.

The End of the Abbey

John Palmer, the abbot, was the first abbot in the county to surrender. The abbey, which had seven canons at this point, was dissolved in 1536 and the buildings were demolished. The lands were given to Thomas Audeley and then bought by Henry Maynard. Excavations in 1949 revealed the infirmary, to the east of the church.

Spooks: the Ghostly Monk

According to legend, one of the monks was decapitated by King John's army in the conflict of 1215. A ghost appeared for many years afterwards, especially around the

Cherry Lane area. In the 1940s, a decapitated skeleton was dug up in the grounds under a thirteenth-century stone coffin lid – and the monk hasn't been seen since.

Tunnels

There was allegedly a tunnel between the abbey and Horham Hall, three miles away. However, there's no evidence of a tunnel nowadays, and most of the alleged tunnels at monastic sites turn out to be simple drainage culverts.

Coffins thought to be from Tilty Abbey.
Photograph by author.

Tiptree Priory

Tiptree priory (OS map reference TL875 143) is the remains of an Augustinian priory dedicated to St Mary and St Nicholas. All that can be seen now is a rubble wall extending to the east of the existing house, which was built around 1550; it used to be called Tiptree House, and is now known as The Priory.

The Beginnings of the Priory

The priory was founded by the Tregoz family in the late twelfth century.

Scandals: Throwing the Prior out 'by the legs'. The Kidnapped Prior. Fined for Non-attendance. Rows Over Succession

In 1389, there was trouble at the priory. Prior Thomas Malton complained to the king that the patron, John de Boys, had thrown him out 'by the legs'. He was given a grant of protection for two years – but, only a month later, the bishop revoked the grant, saying that the prior had told lies to get protection and stop the bishop exercising his jurisdiction. However, a later prior claimed that John de Boys had deprived him of rents for a long time, and asked de Boys' executors for restitution.

In 1411, prior John Leghes took Elming Leget and his wife Alice to court, saying that they'd kidnapped him on 12 February and taken him to Great Braxted, then to Black Notley, imprisoning him in both places. Leget said that Leghes was one of their bondmen from the manor of Chatham, but the prior proved that he was a freeman and they'd acted illegally. The Legets had to pay the prior 60s in damages (equivalent to just over £1100 in modern terms).

At the Augustinian Chapter in 1443, Tiptree was fined 3s 4d for not sending representatives to the chapter.

There was another row in 1515 when the prior, William Barlow, resigned. The patron, Anthony Darcy, argued that he had the right to appoint Barlow's successor as he was the lord of Tollehunt Tregoz; however, the bishop argued that the bishop had appointed the priors for years. It had to go to arbitration, where Dr Walter Stone and serjeant-at-law Richard Broke decided that Darcy should choose the prior, but out of respect to the bishop he could choose the prior at the next two vacancies.

The End of the Priory

The priory was suppressed in 1525. Revenues were given to Wolsey's college, Oxford.

Waltham Abbey

Waltham Abbey (OS map reference TL38270066) is the remains of an Augustinian abbey dedicated to the Holy Cross. Only the Norman nave of the abbey church remains, which is used as the parish church (i.e. the Church of the Holy Cross and St Lawrence). The remains of the gatehouse, bridge and fishponds are nearby.

The Beginnings of the Priory

The story of the beginnings of the priory is told in a manuscript, *De Inventione Sanctæ Crucis Nostræ*, which was written in the twelfth century by one of the monks at the abbey. A man had a vision in Montacute, Somerset; as a result of his dream, he found a miraculous cross. The cross was apparently life-size, made of stone, and the cart containing it couldn't move until the name of Waltham was mentioned.

(However, there was a religious house at Nazeing, near Waltham, which ended at the time of the Viking invasions, and it's possible that their treasures were carried to Montacute and buried there.)

Tovi, who was a wealthy landowner and one of Canute's chief thegns and the king's standard-bearer, built a church at Waltham to house the cross and appointed two priests to watch over it.

Waltham Abbey; plate from Thomas Kitson Cromwell's Excursions Through Essex, *1818-9.*

Refoundation by King Harold

In 1060, Harold Godwineson refounded the abbey as a secular college with 12 priests and a dean, Wlwin. The main teacher at the college was Athelard, who was originally sent to cure Harold of paralysis with the help of the holy cross of Waltham. Athelard also helped Harold to set up the laws and customs of the college.

After Harold was defeated by William the Conqueror in 1066, William took part of their college's lands but left the monks alone; William II interfered a little more, and took some of their most valuable goods to Caen. Henry I gave the abbey to his queen, Maud.

Waltham Abbey gateway. Photograph by author.

The Burial of King Harold

There is a stone at the abbey to mark what might be the final resting place of Harold Godwineson. However, there's no proof; and it was also thought that he was buried at the Sussex coast. Within a century of the Conquest, rumours sprang up that Harold didn't die at Battle.

Gerald of Wales, writing in 1188, said that Harold lived as an anchorite at Chester; others said that Henry I visited the hermit and on his deathbed said that the hermit was Harold. The Life of Harold, written in the early thirteenth century, says that when Harold was wounded at the Battle of Hastings he was carried to Winchester and a Saracen woman nursed him. Apparently, he went to seek allies abroad, but failed, and went on a pilgrimage for his sin of breaking an oath – in other words, supporting the claim depicted on the Bayeux Tapestry that Harold swore an oath on relics that he would not oppose William. After the pilgrimage, he came back to Dover and eventually went in disguise to Wales. On his deathbed, in Chester, he confessed his true identity.

The Icelandic sagas also say that Harold lived after the Battle of Hastings; and Ralph

Statue of Harold at Waltham Abbey.
Photograph by author.

Memorial to Harold at Waltham Abbey. The gravestone reads:
This stone marks the position
of the high altar
behind which King Harold
is said to have been buried
1066

Photograph by author.

of Coggeshall says that abbot of Waltham asked Harold's younger brother Gyrth, who was very old, if they had the king's body, and Gyrth said, 'You have not Harold.'

So was Harold buried at Sussex, Waltham or Chester? It's something we're unlikely ever to know for sure, though the monastic chronicle at Waltham is very clear that his body was buried there; according to the chronicle, between 1124 and 1177 his body was moved three times during building work in the church.

Civil War: Burning Down the Abbey

In 1144, during the civil war between Matilda and Stephen, Geoffrey de Mandeville burned Waltham; the villagers brought their valuables to the church for safe-keeping, but Mandeville's men invaded the church. The fire had spread to the canons' houses, and although they asked his men to stop – particularly as they believed that Mandeville, as the Earl of Essex, was their protector – the men refused. In desperation, according to the chronicler, the monks dragged the Holy Cross from above the altar, begging for help, and threw it on the ground; and at that exact moment Geoffrey received his death wound at the Siege of Burwell. Geoffrey certainly died from a head wound, unshriven, in 1144 (see Walden and Pleshey for more details). More than that, the chronicler stated that five Flemish mercenaries, who had been working for Mandeville and had filled their sacks with treasures, were suddenly so confused that they couldn't find their way out of the church. The monks gave the mercenaries a severe flogging and then set them free; their leader, Humphrey de Barrington, who had entered the church on horseback and incited his men to plunder, became mad as he left the town and was carried back to the church, where he died three days later – after repenting his behaviour and giving the church fourteen acres of land.

Refoundation by Henry II: Penance for the Death of Thomas Becket

Henry II and Thomas Becket, the Archbishop of Canterbury, came to blows over the Constitutions of Clarendon, where Henry aimed to restrict the power of the church and the Pope while reforming civil law. One in six people in the country were lay clergymen, not priests, but could claim 'benefit of clergy' and be tried in a church court for any crimes – where they would usually receive a much lighter sentence than if they'd been tried in a civil court. Henry wanted these 'criminous clerks' to be tried in a civil court, which he saw as restoring order after the civil war between Stephen and Matilda. He proposed a solution that if a church court convicted someone of murder, the criminal should be deprived of the church's protection and the punishment should be set by the civil court. Becket saw this as undermining the whole concept of clerical immunity – once someone was handed over to the civil courts, he was effectively no longer a clerk.

At Clarendon, Becket told his bishops that they had to sign Henry's proposals – but Becket himself then dressed as a penitent, sentenced himself to a fast and repented of the oath. Becket's letters say that he told the bishops to sign so that Henry's wrath would be diverted from them – but he intended to continue opposing the proposals himself.

In 1164 Henry summoned Becket to a trial at Northampton, accusing him of embezzling £300 while he was Lord Chancellor. Becket denied the charges but wanted the matter settled quickly, so he offered to pay the £300. Henry accused him of treason, and Becket said that the court had no right to judge him because he was a clerk. Becket left for France, where he thought he'd be safe. Henry promptly sequestered all his property and issued edicts against his supporters.

Becket had almost persuaded the Pope to excommunicate Henry; and then Henry got the Archbishop of York to crown Henry the Young King (Henry II's second son). Coronations

Waltham Abbey.
Photograph by author.

were a right of the Archbishop of Canterbury, and Becket was furious. He agreed a compromise with the king that he would return to England and re-crown Henry the Younger – but the prince refused to meet Becket (despite the fact that Becket had also looked after the prince in his own home – it was the custom at the time that the children of noble houses were fostered out to other nobles – and at one point Henry the Younger was closer to Becket than he was to his own father).

Becket began excommunicating everyone who had opposed him – including the Archbishop of York and the bishops of London and Salisbury. Henry, at the winter court in Normandy, was furious, and demanded to know who would rid him of this troublesome priest. It was probably a cry of frustration, but the king's words were taken as a royal command. So four of his knights travelled back to England. So the story goes, they rode to Canterbury Cathedral. They met Becket and demanded that he should go back to France with them and account to the King for his actions. Becket refused. The next day, 29 December 1170, they tried to drag him out of the cathedral, and he resisted. The knights struck him with their swords – also severely injuring Edward Grim, a visiting monk from Cambridge who tried to protect Becket and later wrote an eyewitness account of the event. However, Becket stood firm; at the next blow he fell to his knees, saying, 'For the name of Jesus and the protection of the Church, I am ready to embrace death.' Le Bret thrust his sword so hard through Becket's head that the sword broke on the cathedral floor – and rather gruesomely, according to Grim, '[Becket's] crown, which was large, separated from his head so that the blood turned white from the brain yet no less did the brain turn red from the blood; it purpled the appearance of the church with the colours of the lily and the rose.' Becket – who was wearing a hair shirt underneath his habits – had become a martyr.

The pope excommunicated the four knights and banned Henry from taking mass until he'd made reparation for his sin. Three years after his death, Becket was canonised, and Henry II made public penance at Becket's tomb, the following year. Becket's tomb became the most popular pilgrimage site in England; but the problem of 'criminous clerks' continued until the Reformation.

Henry II had vowed to build an abbey in honour of Thomas Becket as part of his penance, and decided that the cheapest way to do it was to overthrow Harold's foundation at Waltham, get rid of the secular canons and put Augustinian canons in their place. In 1177, he claimed that the canons were immoral (they weren't, but some of them were married), and the Pope gave him licence to convert the college into a priory. The first prior was Ralph; when Waltham became an abbey in 1184, Walter de Gant became the first abbot. Henry paid a lot of money towards rebuilding the church – a process that went on for 50 years. A hospital was built within the precincts in 1218 and the church was rededicated in 1242 by William, the bishop of Norwich.

Plague and rebellions

The abbey suffered badly from the plague in the fourteenth century. It also suffered during the Uprising of 1381, when many of its documents were burned. On St Bartholomew's Day in 1410, the abbey was attacked and forcibly entered by villagers from Loughton, who insulted the abbot and hit the sheriff. A pardon was granted. In 1423 many bondsmen rebelled again and refused to perform their usual services for the abbey.

The End of the Abbey

The abbey was dissolved on 23 March 1540, and was the last monastic house in the country to surrender.

Scandals: Fight Between Town and Gown

There was a fight between the abbot and the town about the marshes. The only documented source of the fight, however, is unreliable because it was written by the monks. According to them, in 1248 the townsfolk came onto the marsh, killed four of the abbot's horses and drove away the rest. The following year, the townsfolk told him to take his mares and colts off the marsh; the abbot said that he would give them an answer in a week's time but had to go on business to Lincoln. While he was away, the townsfolk drove the horses off the marshes, drowning three and wounding ten, and beat the keepers. On the abbot's return, they offered him damages; but, the following day, they went to the king and complained that the abbot was trying to drive them off the marsh. The abbot promptly excommunicated them; they took him to court, but lost.

Scandals: Trapped in a Buck Stall

According to Fuller's church history, the monks used to visit the nuns at Cheshunt. Sir Henry Colt was one of Henry VIII's favourite noblemen and decided to play a trick on the monks. He put a 'buck stall' (which was an enclosure for trapping deer) in the narrowest part of the marshes and got his friends to trap the monks as they came back from the nunnery. He presented them to Henry VIII, the next day, and Henry said that he had 'often seen sweeter but never fatter venison'!

Spooks

Plainchant has been heard in the area and lights have been seen in the building when nobody was there. Monks have also been seen walking in the graveyard, and the area is meant to be haunted by a girl who killed herself to avoid a priest's attentions.

Wix Priory

Wix Priory (OS map reference TM 1648 2909) is the remains of a Benedictine nunnery dedicated to St Mary. The remains include the west wall and the north arcade of the present church of St Mary the Virgin, which was built from the ruins of the priory church in 1744.

The Beginnings of the Priory

The priory, for eight to ten nuns, was founded in 1125-35 by Walter Mascherell, Alexander de Waham and Edith, the children of Walter the deacon; Walter owned much of Wix in the eleventh century. King Stephen also granted the nuns permission to keep 'two greyhounds and four braches' to hunt hares in the forest of Essex.

Clearly the nuns were very poor, because in 1193 the pope gave a bull promising indulgences to those who helped the nuns, as their revenues weren't enough to keep them. However, the nuns had a whole dossier of forged documents by the end of the twelfth century, including five Episcopal charters; the papal bull has pincer marks at the top, showing where the laces had been reinserted. (However, there is a possibility that some of these documents replaced original charters that had been damaged.)

The Uprising of 1381

During the uprising of 1381, the villagers attacked the priory and burned the court rolls (which said what services they owed to the priory, including labour). The prioress promptly evicted them and fined them before allowing them back into their lands.

Scandal: the Prioress of Redlingfield

Clearly discipline at the nunnery was good – to the point where a prioress who'd behaved very badly was sent there to do her penance.

Arcades on the north wall of St Mary's church, Wix. Photograph by author.

On 9 September 1427, Thomas Ryngstede, the dean of the college of St Mary in the Fields in Norwich, was sent by the Bishop of Norwich to do the visitation of Redlingfield Nunnery. Isabel Hermyte, the prioress, confessed that on 25 January 1425 she'd promised on oath to observe the bishop's injunctions – but since then she'd never been to confession, and she hadn't observed Sundays or principal feasts. She also admitted that she and one of her novices, Joan Tates, had slept in a private chamber instead of in the dormitory with the other nuns; that she only had nine nuns instead of thirteen in the community; and there was only one chaplain instead of three.

Financially, too, she was in trouble; as with many priors, she hadn't done her annual accounts. She also admitted to taking goods, and having trees cut down and selling them without telling the rest of the convent or getting their consent.

Personally, she was accused of 'laying violent hands on Agnes Brakle on St Luke's Day' – but, far worse, she was 'de incontinentia scandalizata' with Thomas Langelond, the bailiff (in other words, she'd slept with him). She'd been alone with him in 'private and suspicious places', including a small hall with all the windows closed and 'sub heggerow' (i.e. underneath the hedgerow!).

Ryngstede's judgement was that they were all as bad as each other. He ordered that the whole convent should fast on Fridays, only having bread and beer. Joan Tates had admitted to incontinence, so she had go to in front of the convent the following Sunday, dressed in white flannel and wearing no veil. Isabel's confession was written in the diocesan register, and she was banished to the priory of Wix.

It's not recorded whether she behaved any better at Wix…

Scandals: Frippery

At the visitation of 1509, it was clear that the nuns were used to entertainment and liked nice clothes and fripperies, because the bishop's injunction said that the nuns would be excommunicated if they allowed public spectacles (defined as 'seculars, javelin-play, dances or trading in the streets or open spaces of Wix'). They were also not allowed to visit anywhere or go on pilgrimage without permission from the diocese, and were forbidden to wear hairpins made of silver or gilt, or 'kirtles' made of fustian or worsted.

The End of the Priory

The priory was dissolved in 1525 to fund of Wolsey's college at Oxford; it was the largest of the six Essex priories dissolved by Wolsey. It was dissolved by his agent John Alen on 1 March 1525 and the three nuns and prioress were transferred elsewhere. The buildings were then demolished, including the convent church; Abbey Farmhouse was built on the site at some time before 1575.

Excavations

In 1961 a stone coffin was discovered during ploughing nearby; the lid had a decorative cross showing Saxon influences which dated it to around 1140. It contained a large skeleton which was thought to belong to Alexander, one of the founders of the priory. Excavations showed the footings of the nunnery, and a ground survey in 1994 showed the position of other buildings, including the chapter house and what's thought to be the infirmary.

Spooks: the Bell Cage

There's a story that the bell in the cage in Wix churchyard belonged to the nunnery. Apparently the tower of the nuns' church was built three times, and each time the devil pulled it down until they put the bell in a cage to stop him.

The present bell cage, made by the late Roger Paskell, dates from 1975, when an attempt was made to steal the bell.

Bell cage next to St Michael's church, Wix. Photograph by author.

Selected Bibliography

James Bettley and Nikolaus Pevsner, *The Buildings of England: Essex*, Yale University Press 2007, ISBN 9780300116144

Duffield William Coller, *The People's History of Essex*, Chelmsford, 1861

Thomas Kitson Cromwell, *Excursions Through Essex*, 2 volumes, London 1818-9

William Dugdale, *Monasticon Anglicanum*, 1817

F. Donald Logan, *Runaway Religious in Medieval England*, Cambridge University Press 2002, ISBN 9780521520225

David Neville, *Lost Castles of Essex*, Ian Henry Publications 2003, ISBN 0860255204

Philip Morant, *The History and Antiquities of the County of Essex*, 2 volumes, 1769

George Parkyns, *Monastic and baronial remains*, London 1816

James Sargant Storer, *The Antiquarian and Topographical Cabinet*, London, 1807

Michael Swanton (trans), *The Anglo-Saxon Chronicles*, Phoenix 1996, ISBN 1842120034

Jennifer Westwood and Jacqueline Simpson, *The Lore of the Land*, Penguin 2005, ISBN 9780141007113

Thomas Wright, *The History and Topography of Essex*, London 1831